JEFFERSON *and* MONROE

CONSTANT FRIENDSHIP *and* RESPECT

JEFFERSON
and
MONROE

CONSTANT FRIENDSHIP *and* RESPECT

by Noble E. Cunningham, Jr.

Preface by Joyce Appleby

THOMAS JEFFERSON FOUNDATION

Monticello Monograph Series

2003

Library of Congress Cataloging-in-Publication Data

Cunningham, Noble E., 1926-
  Jefferson and Monroe : constant friendship and respect / by Noble E.
Cunningham, Jr. ; preface by Joyce Appleby.
      p. cm. -- (Monticello monograph series)
Includes bibliographical references and index.
  ISBN 1-882886-21-6 (alk. paper)
  1. Jefferson, Thomas, 1743-1826. 2. Monroe, James, 1758-1831. 3.
Presidents--United States--Biography. 4. Friendship--United
States--Case studies. 5. United States--Politics and
government--1775-1783. 6. United States--Politics and
government--1783-1865. I. Title. II. Series.

E332.2 .C86 2003
973.5'4'092--dc21

                                                                    2003044657

ON THE COVER

Detail from *Thomas Jefferson* by Rembrandt Peale, 1800 (the White House collection, courtesy of
the White House Historical Association); detail from *James Monroe* by Gilbert Stuart, 1817. Oil on
wood. 26⅝ x 21½ in. [67.6 x 54.6 cm]. Acc. no: 1900.4. (Courtesy of the Pennsylvania Academy of
the Fine Arts, Philadelphia. Pennsylvania Academy Purchase). In background, draft of letter from
Thomas Jefferson to James Monroe, October 24, 1823 (courtesy Library of Congress).

Copyright © 2003 by Thomas Jefferson Foundation, Inc.

Designed by Gibson Design Associates.
Edited and coordinated by Beth L. Cheuk.

This book was made possible by support from the
Martin S. and Luella Davis Publications Endowment.

Distributed by
The University of North Carolina Press
Chapel Hill, North Carolina 27515-2288
1-800-848-6224

CONTENTS

From Medals of the First Sixteen Presidents *by George Hampden Lovett (New York, 1861).*

PREFACE

No other state can match Virginia's singular role in America's nation building during the first fifty years after Independence. Thomas Jefferson crafted the Continental Congress's Declaration of Independence. George Washington led the Continental Army to victory over Great Britain, against great odds. George Mason's Bill of Rights for Virginia became the model for other states. James Madison drafted the Virginia plan for the Philadelphia Constitutional Convention, which became the basis for the United States Constitution.

To top off this splendid record, once the Constitution went into force, Virginians occupied the presidency through eight of the first nine four-year terms. And in the midst of this sequence, Jefferson and Madison created America's first opposition party.

The Civil War, with its long coda for a defeated South, has obscured just what a powerhouse Virginia was in the early Republic. The state was larger and wealthier than the next two states combined. But the virtuosity of their leaders can't be attributed to material factors alone. Something more protean was involved, and Noble Cunningham's fine study of Jefferson and James Monroe, the last of Virginia's revolutionary presidents, gives us some clues about what it was.

Virginia's grandees—the politically savvy, great planters—learned in the seventeenth century the importance of being skillful in governing if they were to protect their estates against the incursions from the Mother Country. Politics also supplied a stage upon which to display their intellectual and social gifts. Theirs was not a democratic order, but rather a grand gentlemen's club to which plain farmers deferred as long as the men they sent to the House of Burgesses served the good of Virginia as a whole.

Tactics learned in the colonial era endured. The pertinent one here was the speedy identification of youthful talent. Nothing served Virginia better than nurturing those youths in their midst who displayed the kind of critical intelligence and social graces necessary to secure Virginia's prosperity. Where a meritocracy must wait for people to demonstrate their merit, Virginia's gentleman planters had their eye out for budding talent. Madison had been elected to the Virginia Assembly when he was nineteen. Jefferson spotted the twenty-one-year-old James Monroe's virtues when he came to read law with him in 1780. Then governor, Jefferson opened up more than the law books for Monroe.

Both men served together in the Continental Congress and shared lodgings for five months before Jefferson left to serve as American minister to France. This intimacy seems to have sealed their closeness. During the ensuing five years, they wrote each other frequently, Monroe regularly satisfying Jefferson's curiosity about the play of politics at home. Monroe's service in the Virginia legislature and Continental Congress brought out the conservative side of his dichotomous political personality. Strongly impressed with the local interests of Virginians, he became an anti-Federalist during the nine months that the draft Constitution for the United States was being debated up and down the Atlantic coast. Jefferson, loyal to James Madison, supported the Constitution from his post in Paris.

Jefferson and Monroe were destined to move onto the national scene once the new government was formed under Washington. Jefferson came back from France to discover that he had been named the first secretary of state. Monroe joined him in Philadelphia when he became one of Virginia's senators in 1790. His original anti-Federalism predisposed him to be critical to the Federalists' centralizing tendencies. Monroe shared Jefferson's impulsive hostility to Hamilton's fiscal program, though it was Madison who most helped Jefferson transform random concerns over policies into an effective opposition party. Of more immediate consequence to Jefferson and Monroe's personal friendship, Monroe bought land near Monticello to build a home to be closer to his patron.

The French Revolution, which erupted just as Washington was forming his government, plunged Europe into war. From 1791 to the Battle of Waterloo in 1815, the protracted hostilities between France and England embroiled the United States in endless conflicts over searches on the high seas, blockades, seizures, and the

English practice of "impressing" into service those captured American sailors thought to be British deserters. Washington, like Jefferson, recognized Monroe's abilities and named him minister to France in 1794. Sharing Jefferson's enthusiasm for the French revolutionary ideals of "liberty, fraternity, and equality," Monroe faced a difficult task in representing an administration that increasingly favored the British in this titanic, European struggle.

Much ink has been spilled scrutinizing Jefferson's personality. Less attention has been paid to Monroe's. Yet in public, he oscillated between impulse and caution. Considered by some a trimmer, Monroe could also act with what seems like uncharacteristic passion. When he arrived in Paris as American minister, for instance, the government was absorbed in one of its many reconfigurations. Impatient to be formally received, Monroe spontaneously went to a session of the Convention to declare his and his country's admiration for France.

After two years, Washington recalled Monroe in something of a rebuke for his French sympathies, provoking Monroe to publish a public vindication of his service. When Jefferson became president, Monroe was governor of Virginia. Jefferson's presidency was to be plagued by similar hassles with the European belligerents, no doubt drawing the two men still further together. Eager to buy New Orleans in 1803, Jefferson sent Monroe to help the American minister in France. This surely was the happiest hour in Monroe's rather checkered diplomatic career. Together Monroe and Robert R. Livingston decided to act beyond their instructions and accept Napoleon's offer to sell the entire Louisiana Territory.

Despite the assumption that Madison would succeed Jefferson as president, a group of Virginians put up Monroe's name in 1808. Jefferson and Monroe remained steadfast friends through this awkward period, and Monroe's tactful behavior soon won back Madison's friendship. In 1811, he joined Madison's cabinet as secretary of state, winning the kind of public acclaim that secured him the presidency after Madison's two terms.

The twenty-four-year occupation of the White House by Jefferson and his two closest friends guaranteed the triumph of the Republicans' program to democratize American society and limit the scope of federal power. Nothing like it was ever to be repeated. Tied to a slave system which the North abjured, Virginia lost its ascendancy in the next few decades, but no other state can match its shaping influence on the early republic.

— JOYCE APPLEBY

University of California
Los Angeles

INTRODUCTION

*T*homas Jefferson and James Monroe are remembered for their close ties, whether political, geographical, intellectual, or emotional. Politically they were connected as like-minded Republicans who served in many of the same key political offices in Virginia, within the federal government, or even abroad in France. They were linked geographically not only by the fact that that each claimed Virginia as home but also because, at Jefferson's urging, Monroe acquired property a few miles from Monticello. Intellectually, they grappled with the same issues and shared similar passions on a national and personal scale, such as their pivotal participation in the purchase of Louisiana and in the creation of the University of Virginia. Emotionally, their letters reveal a rich friendship that altered and grew over the years.

Rather than a dual biography, this work focuses on the lives of Jefferson and Monroe when their paths crossed and particularly on their roles in shaping the early American republic. Both men have been the subjects of detailed biographies, and each has figured prominently in other writings on early American history. Jefferson—senior to Monroe in both age and accomplishment, and as the author of the Declaration of Independence—early gained a prominent place in the young nation's history. Meanwhile, Monroe risked his life as a young soldier in the American Revolutionary army.

In his early relationship with Jefferson, Monroe stood in the shadow of his mentor. Jefferson, however, soon placed Monroe as an equal, and, as time passed, their friendship strengthened and endured. To trace their relationship and actions during the critical early years of the American republic broadens and deepens insights into the formative years of the United States of America.

— NOBLE E. CUNNINGHAM, JR.

Thomas Jefferson *by*
Rembrandt Peale, 1800
(the White House collection,
courtesy of the White House
Historical Association);
James Monroe *by Gilbert*
Stuart, 1817 (courtesy of the
Pennsylvania Academy of
the Fine Arts, Pennsylvania.
Pennsylvania Academy
Purchase, Acc. no: 1900.4)

Chapter I

1776-1795

As far as the historical record reveals, the lives of Thomas Jefferson and James Monroe first crossed sometime late in the year 1779 or early in 1780. It was a low time for Americans in the Revolutionary War against Great Britain. Jefferson, who would gain lasting fame as the principal author of the American Declaration of Independence, was then governor of Virginia. Monroe, fifteen years younger than Jefferson, had left the College of William and Mary to join the Revolutionary Army in 1776. Before his nineteenth birthday, Monroe, as a young lieutenant, was seriously wounded in the battle of Trenton in December 1776. By 1779, Monroe was a major, but without troops to command; he returned to Virginia, where the Assembly appointed him lieutenant colonel to command a regiment of militia expected to be raised. When the needed troops were not enlisted, Monroe re-entered the College of William and Mary and began to read law under Governor Jefferson in Williamsburg. After the Virginia capital moved from Williamsburg to Richmond in 1780, Monroe accepted Jefferson's suggestion that he move to Richmond and continue reading law with him.

On June 10, 1780, on behalf of the Governor's Council, Governor Jefferson sent Monroe a note: "The Executive have occasion to employ a gentleman in a confidential business, requiring great discretion, and some acquaintance with military things. They wish you to undertake it if not inconsistent with your present pursuits. It will call you off some weeks, to the distance of a couple hundred miles. Expences will be borne and a reasonable premium. Will you be so good as to attend us immediately for further communications."[1]

Monroe promptly accepted the assignment, and within the week Jefferson sent him instructions detailing a plan to create, through a series of horsemen stationed about forty miles apart, a form of "express" mail between the two men. Monroe would be stationed in "the vicinity of the British army in Carolina where you will continue yourself, observing their movements and when their importance requires it, communicating them to me." Jefferson noted that "The state and resources of our friends, their force, the disposition of the people, the prospect of provisions, ammunition, arms, and other circumstances, the force and condition of the enemy, will also be proper items of communication."[2]

On the same day, Jefferson wrote to Abner Nash, governor of North Carolina, informing him of the arrangements he made for express communication with Monroe, and offering him the opportunity to take advantage of the system:

> The tardiness and uncertainty of intelligence from the Southern states, and the very interesting situation of things there at present have induced me to send Colo. Monroe, a sensible, judicious, and confidential person, to the neighborhood of the hostile army, for the purpose of collecting and communicating notice of their movements.... I thought it proper to inform your Excellency of this measure, as well because it might afford you a ready and safe conveyance for any communications with which you may please to honour me, more especially if you should think proper to establish a similar line of communication with Colo. Monroe, as that I might recommend that gentleman to your patronage, aid and confidence.[3]

On June 26, 1780, ten days after receiving his orders from Governor Jefferson, Monroe sent his first report to Jefferson. Writing from Cross-Creek, North Carolina, where he had arrived a few days earlier, he explained the lines of communication he had arranged. He also noted his good fortune in meeting with Governor Nash. Monroe reported on good authority the embarkation of a large British force—estimated to number some six thousand men—that had sailed from Charleston, South Carolina. Although the objective of the force could only be conjectured, Monroe noted, the prevailing supposition was that the troops would land somewhere in Virginia.[4] This turned out to be a miscalculation, for the British expedition sailed to New York.

None of Monroe's subsequent reports sent to Jefferson during this mission are known to have survived. Monroe was back in Richmond in early September when he wrote to thank Jefferson for trusting him with the mission:

> Your kindness and attention to me in this and a variety of other instances has realy put me under such obligations to you that I fear I shall hardly ever have it in my power to repay them.... A variety of disappointments ... previous to my acquaintance with your Excellency ... perplexed my plan of life and exposed me to inconveniences which nearly destroyed me.... In this situation you became acquainted with me and undertook the direction of my studies and believe me I feel that whatever I am at present in the opinion of others or whatever I may be in future has greatly arose from your friendship.... The attention your Excellency and Council paid me in calling on me to perform the duties of so important a trust at so critical a time... did me honour and gave me more pleasure than any pecuniary compensation I could possibly derive from it.

Monroe, in fact, received small compensation for his services, writing that "During the greater part of my service in the army I had not my expences borne and as in this instance I have only acted the part which the opinion of the duty I owe to the publick dictated."[5]

During the remainder of the Revolutionary War, Monroe saw only minor military service. He offered his services for the siege of Yorktown, but there were no unfilled officers' posts. Anticipating the end of the war, Monroe conferred with Jefferson about continuing his studies abroad and made arrangements to sail to France in November 1781.[6]

Jefferson's term as governor was scheduled to end on June 2; however, before the Virginia legislature could elect his successor, the invading British army forced the delegates to retreat beyond the Blue Ridge Mountains. Jefferson assumed he was relieved from duties as wartime governor and took his family to the safety of his farm, Poplar Forest, in southern Virginia. He did not return to Monticello until mid-summer, and it was October before he wrote regarding Monroe's projected journey to France for study abroad: "With respect to the part of France or even of Europe in which it will be best for you to reside you will certainly be the best judge yourself, when you get there." Jefferson discussed the merits of Paris and the South of France, reviewed publications that would "afford… agreeable and useful employment," and advised Monroe to "attend Westminster Hall a term or two" along with "an attendance on Parliament," noting that the experiences and the books "may be of use to when you shall become a parliamentary man, which for my country and not for your sake, I shall wish to see you." Jefferson continued, "I shall be very happy to hear from you whenever you can spare time to write, tho' can not promise a full return of American news, secluded as I am and mean to be from the news-taking world."[7]

With his letter to Monroe, Jefferson included several letters for Benjamin Franklin, John Adams, and John Jay—who were in Europe at that time—introducing "Colo. James Monroe who served some time as an officer in the American army and as such distinguished himself in the affair of Princetown as well as on other occasions, having resumed his studies, comes to Europe to complete them. Being a citizen of this state, of abilities, merit and fortune, and my particular friend, I take the liberty of making him known to you."[8]

After a series of disappointments in arranging passage to France, Monroe abandoned his plans to study abroad. Meanwhile, he was elected from King George County to the Virginia House of Delegates. Jefferson, too, was elected to the House after his term as governor had ended, but he declined to accept the post.

Concerned by Jefferson's refusal to serve in the House of Delegates, Monroe relayed the disappointment of his legislative colleagues in a frankly worded letter: "It is publickly said here that the people of your county informed you they had frequently elected you in times of less difficulty and danger than the present to please you, but that now they have called you forth into publick office to serve themselves…. [Y]ou should not decline the service of your country. The present is generally conceived to be an important era which of course makes your attendance particularly necessary."[9]

Jefferson responded at length in a letter defending and justifying his refusal to continue to accept public service. Anxious about his wife's failing health, Jefferson closed his letter, "Mrs. Jefferson has added another daughter to our family. She has been ever since and still continues very dangerously ill."[10]

After the heartbreaking death of his young wife on September 6, 1782, Jefferson slowly began to reorganize his life. His friends rallied to renew a previously rejected appointment as one of the peace commissioners to France. Although he went to Philadelphia in November 1782, Jefferson failed to get passage to France before news reached America that a provisional peace treaty had been signed.

In June 1783, Jefferson was elected by the Virginia legislature as a delegate to the Confederation Congress. Monroe also was chosen as a Virginia delegate to the same Congress, meeting in Annapolis in November. For some five months Monroe and Jefferson shared living quarters, hiring a French chef and dividing expenses.

In May 1784, Congress appointed Jefferson as minister plenipotentiary to join John Adams and Benjamin Franklin in negotiating treaties of amity and commerce in Europe. Before leaving Annapolis, Jefferson sold to Monroe a collection of household items and books that he had acquired there. Numbering some forty-seven volumes—mostly French titles—the books included works by Vattel, Tissot, Chastellux, Blackstone, and Diderot.[11]

Jefferson then wrote a long letter to James Madison in which he added, near the end: "I think Colo. Monroe will be of the Committee of the states. *He wishes a correspondence with you;* and I suppose his situation will render him an useful one to you. The scrupulousness of his honor will make you safe in the most confidential communications. A better man cannot be."[12]

Soon after his appointment, Jefferson hastened to Philadelphia to get his oldest daughter—Martha, then twelve years old—to accompany him to Paris. His younger daughter, Maria, would join him in Paris three years later. While in Philadelphia, Jefferson received a letter from Monroe in which he assured Jefferson, "I shall write you constantly as well before you quit the continent as after."[13] Meanwhile, Jefferson chose William Short, a young Virginia protégé, as his private secretary. He had planned to wait for Short to join him in Boston for the voyage to France, but Short did not arrive before Jefferson sailed on July 5.

When Short left Virginia in July 1784, he carried with him a long letter from Monroe to Jefferson, reporting the latest political and diplomatic news from the United States, although Jefferson would not receive this correspondence until late November. The letter disappointed Jefferson, who had urged his friends and political allies to live near him in Albemarle County, with the news that Monroe had failed in his effort to purchase land near Monticello. At the same time, Monroe assured him: "My failure in this instance will not abate my desire to effect a settlement in that county, it will still form one of my capital objects and will put it in execution as soon as possible."[14] Monroe also discussed his plans for a trip from New York westward through the lakes and rivers.[15]

The letters that passed between Jefferson in France and Monroe in the United States during Jefferson's five years in Paris were frequent and often detailed, revealing a close friendship. In the first letter that Jefferson wrote to Monroe from Paris, he reported that the voyage had been "remarkeably short, being only 19 days from land to land, and I suffered little by sickness." Weather conditions forced the Jeffersons to go ashore at Portsmouth, and it was several days before they took a boat to Le Havre. Continuing in the same letter, Jefferson described the farming area through which they had passed as "a country than which nothing can be more fertile, better cultivated or more elegantly improved."[16]

Writing to Monroe more often than to James Madison, Jefferson not only reported on public affairs in France but also expressed many of his frustrations. "On this side of the Atlantic we are viewed as objects of commerce only," he wrote to Monroe, "and as little to be relied on even for this purpose while it's regulation is so disjointed."[17] High among Jefferson's frustrations were his efforts to live in Paris in a manner comparable to other diplomats despite the meager funds provided by his government, operating under the Articles of Confederation. He explained to Monroe that earlier American ministers to France had been well compensated for their time and expenses, but at the time of his appointment

Congress greatly reduced compensation and made no allowance for the expected diplomatic outfit.[18]

Jefferson also confessed to Monroe, in March 1785: "I have had a very bad winter, having been confined the greatest part of it. A seasoning as they call it is the lot of most strangers: and none I beleive have experienced a more severe one than myself. The air is extremely damp, and the waters very unwholesome."[19] Writing to Madison on the same day, Jefferson mentioned neither the weather nor his health.

To both Monroe and Madison, Jefferson sent copies of his book *Notes on the State of Virginia,* a comprehensive survey of the state's natural, cultural, and political history. Having carried the manuscript of the work with him to Paris, and finding printing costs much cheaper in Paris than in Philadelphia, he had two hundred copies printed in the spring of 1785. In sending the copy to Monroe, Jefferson cautioned him—as he did others to whom he sent copies—not to trust the book to anyone who might make it public. "My reason is," he explained to Monroe, "that I fear the terms in which I speak of slavery and of our constitution may produce an irritation which will revolt the minds of our countrymen against reformation of these two articles, and thus do more harm than good."[20]

Jefferson invited both Madison and Monroe to visit him in Paris in the summer of 1785. In one letter urging Monroe to make the voyage, he argued: "The pleasure of the trip will be less than you expect but the utility greater. It will make you adore your own country, it's soil, it's climate, it's equality, liberty, laws, people and manners. My god! How little do my countrymen know what precious blessings they are in possession of, and which no other people on earth enjoy. I confess I had no idea of it myself."[21]

In a letter urging Madison to visit him in Paris, Jefferson added that he expected Monroe to come.[22] However, neither Madison nor Monroe ever visited Jefferson in Paris. Writing to Jefferson from New York in May 1786, Monroe explained why he would not be coming to Paris: "You will be surprised to hear that I have formed the most interesting connection in human life, with a young Lady in this town. As you know my plan was to visit you before I settled myself. But having formed an attachment to this young Lady (a Miss Kortright, the daughter of a gentleman of respectable character and connections in this state tho' injured in his fortunes by the late war) I have found that I must relinquish all other objects not connected with her. We were married about three months since. I remain here untill the fall at which time we move to Fredericksburg in Virginia where I shall settle for the present ... to enter into the practice of law."[23]

Congratulating Monroe on his marriage, Jefferson wrote: "The interest I feel in every one connected with you will justify my presenting my earliest respects to the lady and of tendering her the homage of my friendship."[24]

In addition to his marriage and move to Fredricksburg, Monroe was leaving Congress, and Jefferson faced the loss of a correspondent to provide the privileged communications that Monroe had supplied. "I know not whom I may venture confidential communications after you are gone," wrote Jefferson in August 1786.[25] Although Monroe planned to begin a law practice in Fredricksburg, he assured Jefferson, "Believe me I have not relinquished the prospect of being your neighbour. The house for which I have requested a plan may possibly be erected near Monticello. To fix there and to have yourself in particular with what friends we may collect around for society is my chief object."[26]

In reply, Jefferson renewed his promise to send Monroe a house plan, and he added: "I wish to heaven you may continue in the disposition to fix it in Albemarle.... Without society, and a society to our taste, humans are never contented."[27] After moving to Fredericksburg and starting his law practice there, Monroe assured Jefferson in the summer of 1787: "I consider my residence here as temporary, merely to serve the purpose of the time, and as looking forward to an establishment somewhere on this side of the mountains, and as convenient as possible to Monticello."[28] From Paris, Jefferson wrote to Monroe that "It would indeed be a most pleasing circumstance to me to see you settle in the neighborhood of Monticello, for thither all my views tend, and not a day passes over my head without looking toward to my return."[29]

One of the first political disagreements between Jefferson and Monroe arose over the issue of ratifying the new Constitution. Unlike James Madison, Monroe was not at the Federal Constitutional Convention of 1787, and he did not support the ratification of the new Constitution by Virginia. Writing to Monroe in August 1788, Jefferson had not yet learned what the vote in Virginia had been, but he declared, "I heartily rejoice that 9 states have accepted the new constitution."[30] The differences of Jefferson and Monroe with respect to the Constitution did not lessen their friendship. Once the Constitution was adopted, Monroe fully supported it, and he was elected to the United States Senate by the Virginia legislature.

In February 1789 Monroe informed Jefferson that he had acquired five hundred acres of land in Albemarle County, Virginia. "It has always been my wish to acquire property near Monticello. I have lately accomplished it." Identifying the location of the land purchased, Monroe continued, "Whether to move up immediately or hereafter when I shall be so happy as to have you as a neighbour I have not yet determined. In any event it puts it within my reach to be contiguous to you when the fatigue of publick life, should dispose you for retirment, and in the interim will enable me in respect to your affairs, as I shall be frequently at Charlottesville as a summer retreat, and in attendance on the district court there, to render you some service."[31]

While Monroe in Virginia was contemplating the time when Jefferson would return to Albemarle County and renew their close friendship, Jefferson was suddenly caught up in one of the most momentous events of his lifetime—the French Revolution. Jefferson was in Paris when the Third Estate proclaimed itself to be the National Assembly of France on June 17, 1789. He was there when the Bastille was stormed on July 14, and Lafayette closely consulted him in drafting the French Declaration of the Rights of Man, proclaimed on August 27.[32]

Although Jefferson was reluctant to leave France during such critical times, he was anxious to return his two daughters to America.[33] They left Paris on September 26, 1789, but because of weather they did not sail from Yarmouth until October 22. With speedy sailing, they arrived in Norfolk on November 23, 1789.

Soon after landing, Jefferson learned for the first time that he had been appointed by President George Washington to be the secretary of state in the new government under the Constitution. Jefferson had anticipated returning to France to watch the momentous, revolutionary changes taking place there. Bowing to the wishes of the president, however, he accepted the appointment as secretary of state on February 14, 1790.

It was March 21 before Jefferson arrived in New York, the temporary capital, to assume his post in the new government that had been in operation for nearly a year. Pressed with the duties of his office, Jefferson found no time to write to Monroe until June 20, when he sent him a detailed report on the proceedings, progress, and problems of the new government. Among the most pressing issues were those relating to the funding of the national debt and fixing the location of the national capital. "The assumption of the state debts has appeared as revolting to several states as their non-assumption to others," Jefferson told Monroe; and the location of the new capital was still undecided.[34] When Jefferson wrote to Monroe on July 11, he was able to report that "The bill for removing the federal government to Philadelphia for 10 years and then to Georgetown has at length past both houses."[35]

While Jefferson became increasingly absorbed with his duties as secretary of state, Monroe also was being drawn back into the political world. Elected to fill the vacancy left by the death of Senator William Grayson, Monroe took the oath of office as a senator from Virginia in December 1790.[36]

With Jefferson as secretary of state and Monroe in the United States Senate, few letters record the views and thoughts that passed between them during the times when they were in the same city. Their correspondence resumed when separated by distance, and in a letter from Monroe in Richmond to Jefferson in Philadelphia, in June 1791, Monroe wrote, "Upon political subjects we perfectly agree, and particularly in the reprobation of all measures that may be calculated to elevate the government above the people, or place it in any respect without its natural boundary. To keep it there nothing is necessary, but virtue in a part only (for in the whole it cannot be expected) of the high publick servants, and a true development of the principles of those acts which have a contrary tendency. The bulk of the people are for democracy, and if they are well informed the ruin of such enterprizes will infallibly follow."[37]

From Williamsburg, Monroe wrote to Jefferson in the summer of 1792: "Whether things have reached their height in the division of parties, relative to government, in America, … seems doubtful. That the partizans for monarchy are numerous and powerful, in point of talents and influence is in my estimation certain…. I am well satisfied the republican scale will prevail, but consider its preponderance by no means as completely established yet."[38]

At the time Monroe wrote this letter, Jefferson was already contemplating retiring as secretary of state at the end of Washington's first term as president in March 1793. Washington, however, persuaded him to continue longer, and Jefferson remained at his post until December 31, 1793. The outbreak of war between Great Britain and France made Jefferson's last months in office difficult, creating problems and raising issues that dominated national politics. Formally resigning on December 31, Jefferson left Philadelphia on January 5, 1794, and returned to Monticello.

After two severe winter months that brought one six-inch snow that lay on the ground for five days and cold temperatures as low as 14 degrees, Jefferson missed being in Philadelphia. "I have never received a letter from Philadelphia since I left it except a line or two once from E[dmund] R[andolph]," Jefferson wrote to Monroe two months after leaving Pennsylvania. He closed the letter by adding, "We have often wondered together, when at Philadelphia, what our friends here could mean by saying they had nothing to write about. You now see that there is nothing but complaints for want of information—for want of commerce, —weather—crops and such things as you are too little of a farmer to take much interest in."[39]

Meanwhile, on March 3, Monroe sent Jefferson a long letter that would not reach Monticello until March 31. Monroe began by writing, "The avidity with which I knew you sought retirement and peace, undisturbed by political occurrences, with the further consideration that no event of any importance had taken place since you left us, prevented my trespassing on you sooner. I am perfectly satisfied you will find in retirement a contentment and tranquility not to be hoped for in publick life…. I look forward with pleasure to the period, and it shall be no distant one, when I shall occupy as your neighbour the adjoining farm."[40]

Neither Jefferson nor Monroe at this time could anticipate the course of events that would engage both men in public life for many years to come. Indeed, a new call to Monroe came only a few months later. As the session of Congress was drawing to a close, on May 27, 1794, President Washington nominated James Monroe to be the United States minister to France—the post earlier filled by Jefferson. The Senate confirmed Monroe's nomination the next day.

Informing Jefferson of his reaction to being asked by Secretary of State Edmund Randolph if he would accept the appointment, Monroe wrote: "The proposition as you will readily conceive surprised me, for I really thought I was among the last men to whom it would be made, and so observed." He added that Randolph told him the president was resolved to send a Republican to France and that both James Madison and Robert R. Livingston had refused the position.[41]

Monroe promptly accepted the appointment and hastily made arrangements to leave for Paris. There was no time even to visit Jefferson before departing. In mid-June 1794, Monroe, his wife, and daughter sailed from Baltimore. With fine weather, they made a speedy twenty-nine-day Atlantic crossing and reached Paris on August 2.[42]

The Monroes arrived in France as the Reign of Terror was coming to an end. Writing a long letter to Jefferson from Paris on September 7, 1794, Monroe reported that the press of duties had kept him from writing any previous private letters to America. He explained: "It happened that I took my station a few days after Robertspierre had left his in the Convention, by means of the guillitin, so that every thing was in commotion, as was natural upon such an event; but it was the agitation of universal joy occasioned by a deliverance from a terrible oppression and which had pervaded every part of the Republick. After encountering some serious difficulties growing out of the existing state of things, I was presented to the Convention and recognized."[43]

Although Jefferson received Monroe's letter on December 16, it was May 26, 1795, before he answered it, when he confessed, "it would be difficult to say why this is the first time I have written to you. Revising the case myself, I am sensible it has proceeded from that sort of procrastination which so often takes place when no circumstance fixes a business to a particular time. I have never thought it possible through the whole time that I should be ten days longer without writing you, and thus more than a year has run off." He then offered an update on political matters, noting, "I am too much withdrawn from the scene of politics to give you any thing in that line worth your notice." Even so, he discussed the suppression of what has come to be known as the Whiskey Rebellion, when Pennsylvania farmers resisted an excise tax on their only marketable product. At the urging of Alexander Hamilton, a militia of nearly thirteen thousand was raised, and as Jefferson continued to Monroe, "an insurrection was announced and proclaimed and armed against, and marched against, but could never be found." Jefferson expressed his outrage at Hamilton's bold display of military force: "The servile copyist of Mr. Pitt. thought he too must have his alarms, his insurrections and plots against the Constitution. Hence the incredible fact that the freedom of association, of conversation, and of the press, should in the 5th. year of our government have been attacked under the form of a denunciation of the democratic societies, a measure which even England, as boldly as she is advancing to the establishment of an absolute monarchy, has not been bold enough to attempt."[44] Continuing, Jefferson wrote in detail about the plans and projected work for Monroe's house to be built near Jefferson's in Albemarle County.[45]

Monroe had not yet received Jefferson's letter when he wrote to him on June 27, 1795: "I wish much to hear from you having written you several times but received not a line since my appointment here."[46] With his letter Monroe enclosed a lengthy "Sketch of the State of Affairs in France," which he had prepared for publication. A version of this piece was published in the Philadelphia *Aurora* in August 1795, as an "extract from An American gentleman in France."[47]

Writing to Jefferson from Paris in November 1795, Monroe reported that Jefferson's letter of May 26 had not reached him "till lately." After thanking Jefferson for offering to oversee the building of his new house near Monticello, Monroe wrote at length about the new constitution in France. He judged it "defective when tested by those principles which the light of our hemisphere has furnished, yet it is infinitely superior to any thing ever seen before on this side of the Atlantick."[48]

As the United States minister to France, Monroe's reports to Secretary of State Edmund Randolph and to James Madison, a leading figure in the House of Representatives, were more frequent and detailed than his letters to Jefferson at Monticello. Yet Monroe kept in contact, at times sending long, reflective and informative letters to Jefferson at Monticello, such as the following observation: "On this side of the water the scene has greatly changed for the better, in favor of republican government: for since the adoption of the New constitution liberty has as it were been rescued from the dust, where she was trampled under foot by the mob of Paris, whose leaders were perhaps in foreign pay, and restored to the elevated station she ought to hold, and where she is becoming as she ought to be, the idol of the country. France never bore, at any period of her history so commanding a position as she now bears, towards all the powers of Europe, nor did she ever approach it."[49]

Chapter Two

1796-1808

Thomas Jefferson's plans for early retirement ended when he was put forward in 1796 as a candidate for president of the United States. In the close election that followed, Jefferson—coming in second to John Adams—was elected vice president of the United States. Meanwhile, in November 1796, James Monroe had been recalled from his post as minister to France by a dissatisfied President Washington. Upon the arrival of his replacement, Charles Cotesworth Pinckney, Monroe left the post on January 1, 1797. To avoid a winter Atlantic Ocean voyage, Monroe, his wife, and daughter visited Holland and other places in Europe before returning to America.[50] They reached Philadelphia in late June 1797.

The day after the arrival of the Monroes, Jefferson joined Albert Gallatin and Aaron Burr in going aboard ship to welcome them and to demonstrate support for the recalled diplomat. On July 1, Vice President Jefferson also was prominent among some fifty members of Congress, the governor of Pennsylvania, and others who welcomed the return of the Monroes.[51]

Monroe arrived home at a time of high controversy in the press over a private letter that Jefferson had written to Philip Mazzei a year earlier. In that letter—which Jefferson himself had not released to the press—he referred to "an Anglican, monarchical and aristocratical party" that had sprung up in the United States seeking to assimilate the American republic to the British model.[52] Translations of the letter into French and Italian, and back into English, added to the controversy over what Jefferson actually had written. Some readers might conclude that Jefferson had included President Washington among the apostates to republicanism.

When Jefferson sought advice from Madison and Monroe whether to

Thomas Jefferson *by Cornelius Tietbout after Rembrandt Peale. Engraving published by Augustus Day, 1801. (Thomas Jefferson Foundation, Inc.)*

acknowledge publicly the letter, Madison advised against such a course. Monroe, on the other hand, recommended that Jefferson say publicly that he believed the new government under the Constitution was swerving from republican principles. Jefferson followed Madison's advice and remained silent.[53]

Upon Monroe's return to the United States, his mission to France also became a subject of controversy. Monroe did not remain silent. After conferring with Jefferson, he wrote a detailed defense of his service as minister to France, published as *A View of the Conduct of the Executive in the Foreign Affairs of the United States Connected with the Mission to the French Republic During the Years 1794, 5, &6.*[54] "Your book was later coming out than was to have been wished," Jefferson wrote to Monroe in late December 1797, "however it works irresistably. It would be very gratifying to you to hear the unqualified eulogies both on the matter and manner by all who are not hostile to it from principle."[55]

After returning from France, Monroe considered moving to Richmond to practice law, but he decided to remain in Albemarle County and travel to courts in Richmond, Staunton, and Fredericksburg.[56] Jefferson urged Monroe to run for Congress, but Monroe was reluctant to do so. He thanked Jefferson for "the interest you take in what concerns my welfare; of which indeed I have heretofore had so many proofs as long since to have ceased to make acknowledgments."[57] Monroe, however, did not follow Jefferson's advice. At the same time, he did not withdraw from politics, remaining actively involved in Virginia politics and in political activities directed toward the presidential election of 1800.

As that election approached, Jefferson added to a letter to Monroe in January 1799: "P.S. I shall seldom write to you, on account of the strong suspicions of infidelity in the post offices. Always examine the seal before you open my letters, and note whether the impression is distinct."[58] In February 1799, when Jefferson sent Monroe a dozen copies of a political pamphlet by George Nicholas on the laws of the last Congress, he instructed, "I wish you to give these to the most influential characters among our country-men, who are only misled, are candid enough to be open to conviction, and who may have the most effect on their neighbors. It would be useless to give them to persons already sound. Do not let my name be connected with the business."[59]

While actively involved in national politics, Monroe also remained engaged in state political affairs, and on December 6, 1799, he was elected governor of Virginia. In the spring of 1800, as the session of Congress drew to a close, Governor Monroe wrote from Richmond to Vice President Jefferson: "When your presence ceases to be necessary in Philadelphia (and I would certainly remain while it was) your speedy arrival home is what I very much wish. I will arrange things so as to be in Albemarle as soon as I hear you are there."[60]

In late May, presidential candidate Jefferson left Philadelphia to return to Monticello, stepping out of the public eye to allow free discussion of the presidential election being decided in state-by-state votes that would conclude by early December. Before that election was decided, Monroe faced the most serious crisis of his three years as governor of Virginia: a major slave revolt in the city of Richmond and neighboring Henrico County. At the end of August 1800, Gabriel, the slave leader for whom the planned rebellion would be known, organized the uprising, but the plot was discovered and suppressed before it could succeed.[61] To Jefferson, Monroe confided that it was "unquestionably the most serious and formidable conspiracy we have ever known of the kind; tho' indeed to call it so is to give no idea of the thing itself."[62] Jefferson cautioned Monroe against excessive punishment, writing, "Where to stay the hand of the executioner is an important question. Those who have escaped from the immediate danger, must have feelings which would dispose them to extend the executions. Even here, where … a familiarity with slavery, and a possibility of danger from that quarter prepare the general mind for some severities, there is a strong sentiment that there has been hanging enough. The other states and the world at large will forever condemn us if we indulge a principle of revenge, or go one step beyond absolute necessity."[63]

With a presidential election underway, the explosive issue of slavery—so exposed by the slave insurrection in Virginia—was put aside until political waters calmed. The issue, however, continued to reveal the agonizing conflict of slaveholders who opposed slavery but could not find the path to ending it in the United States. Monroe and Jefferson were prominent among that group, discussing alternatives such as the recolonization of American slaves.[64]

When the electoral votes in the presidential election of 1800 were officially counted, following a confusing variety of elections occurring at different times in various states, Jefferson won seventy-three electoral votes, and his chief opponent, Adams, won sixty-five. However, in the hopes of electing Jefferson's fellow Republican Aaron Burr as vice president, all the electors who voted for Jefferson also voted for Burr, producing a tie in the electoral vote. This outcome resulted from the constitutional provision, then in effect, under which each elector cast two votes without distinguishing between president and vice president. The candidate with the highest electoral vote became president, and the second-place candidate became vice president.

The Jefferson-Burr tie vote sent the election to the Federalist-controlled House of Representatives, where voting was by states. Balloting began on February 11, 1801, and the defeated Federalists decided to support the vice presidential candidate, Burr, complicating what might have otherwise been a straightforward decision. On the first ballot Jefferson received the votes of eight states. Burr won six states, and two states were divided. By midnight, nineteen ballots had been taken with no change in the outcome. The deadlock in the voting continued for

The Senate Wing of the Unfinished United States Capitol, Washington, D.C. *by William R. Birch, 1800. (Courtesy of the Library of Congress)*

nearly a week. During the voting, Jefferson reported to Monroe, "Many attempts have been made to obtain terms and promises from me. I have declared to them unequivocally, that I would not receive the government on capitulation, that I would not go into it with my hands tied."[65] Governor Monroe notified Jefferson that if any "plan of usurpation" were attempted, he would immediately convene the Virginia Assembly.[66] Despite this assurance, the peaceful transfer of power was assured on February 17, 1801, when on the thirty-sixth ballot, Jefferson received the votes of ten states and was elected president of the United States. More significant than its convoluted conclusion, the election is momentous since it marks the young republic's first transfer of national power from one party to another.[67]

Governor Monroe was not in Washington on March 4, 1801, for President Jefferson's inauguration—the first to be held in the new capital on the Potomac River. Monroe remained in Richmond for the celebration there on March 4 and ordered the illumination of the city. After reading Jefferson's inaugural address in the newspaper, Monroe wrote to him from Richmond, "Your address has been approved by every description of persons here. It is sound and strong in principle, and grateful to the opposite party. With your judgment, views and principles it is hardly possible you should go wrong. Indeed I count on the good effects of your administration being felt in favor of republican government abroad as well as at home."[68] To James Madison, Monroe commented: "Mr. Jefferson's address delivered on taking the oath gives general satisfaction, as it ought to do. It avows principles which are perfectly sound, and commands the unqualified approbation of the republicans, while it conciliates the opposite party."[69]

Two months after President Jefferson took office, Governor Monroe wrote to him regarding the mode of correspondence between the president and the governors of the states. In a letter to Jefferson on May 4, 1801, Monroe argued that such correspondence should be direct, not through subordinates, explaining, "Before I came into this office I was of opinion that the correspondence between the [president and a governor] should be conducted as between parties that were mutually respectful but equally independent of each other.... Each government is in its sphere sovereign."[70]

SPEECH

OF

THOMAS JEFFERSON, PRESIDENT OF THE UNITED STATES,

DELIVERED

AT HIS INSTALMENT,

MARCH 4, 1801,

AT THE CITY OF WASHINGTON.

FRIENDS, AND FELLOW-CITIZENS,

CALLED upon to undertake the duties of the first executive office of our country, I avail myself of the presence of that portion of my fellow-citizens, which is here assembled, to express my grateful thanks, for the favour with which they have been pleased to look towards me; to declare a sincere consciousness, that the task is above my talents, and that I approach it with those anxious and awful presentiments, which the greatness of the charge, and the weakness of my powers, so justly inspire. A rising nation, spread over a wide and fruitful land....traversing all the seas with the rich productions of their industry....engaged in commerce with nations who feel power and forget right....advancing rapidly to destinies beyond the reach of mortal eye....when I contemplate these transcendent objects, and see the honour, the happiness, and the hopes of this beloved country, committed to the issue and the auspices of this day, I shrink from the contemplation, and humble myself before the magnitude of the undertaking. Utterly, indeed, should I despair, did not the presence of many, whom I here see, remind me, that, in the other high authorities, provided by our constitution, I shall find resources of wisdom, of virtue, and of zeal, on which to rely under all difficulties. To you, then, gentlemen, who are charged with the sovereign functions of legislation, and to those associated with you, I look with encouragement for that guidance and support, which may enable us to steer, with safety, the vessel in which we are all embarked, amidst the conflicting elements of a troubled world.

During the contest of opinion, through which we have past, the animation of discussions and of exertions, has sometimes worn an aspect which might impose on strangers, unused to think freely, and to speak and to write what they think: but this being now decided by the voice of the nation, announced according to the rules of the constitution, all will, of course, arrange themselves under the will of the law, and unite in common efforts, for the common good. All, too, will bear in mind this sacred principle.... that though the will of the majority is, in all cases, to prevail, that will, to be rightful, must be reasonable....that the minority possess their equal rights, which equal laws must protect, and to violate would be oppression. Let us then, fellow-citizens, unite with one heart, and one mind. Let us restore to social intercourse, that harmony and affection, without which, liberty, and even life itself, are but dreary things. And let us reflect, that, having banished from our land, that religious intolerance, under which mankind so long bled and suffered, we have yet gained little, if we countenance a political intolerance, as despotic, as wicked, and capable of as bitter and bloody persecutions.

During the throes and convulsions of the ancient world....during the agonizing spasms of infuriated man, seeking, through blood and slaughter, his long-lost liberty ....it was not wonderful that the agitation of the billows should reach even this distant and peaceful shore,....that this should be more felt and feared by some, and less by others....and should divide opinions as to measures of safety. But every difference of opinion is not a difference of principle. We have called by different names, brethren of the same principle. WE ARE ALL REPUBLICANS; WE ARE ALL FEDERALISTS. If there

be any among us, who would wish to dissolve this union, or to change its republican form, let them stand undisturbed, as monuments of the safety with which error of opinion may be tolerated, where reason is left free to combat it. I know, indeed, that some honest men fear that a republican government cannot be strong....that this government is not strong enough. But would the honest patriot, in the full tide of successful experiment, abandon a government which has so far kept us free and firm, on the theoretic and visionary fear, that this government, the world's best hope, may, by possibility, want energy to preserve itself?....I trust not....I believe this, on the contrary, the strongest government on earth....I believe it the only one, where every man, at the call of the law, would fly to the standard of the law, and would meet invasions of the public order as his own personal concern. Sometimes it is said, that man cannot be trusted with the government of himself. Can he then be trusted with the government of others? Or have we found angels, in the form of kings, to govern him? Let history answer this question.

Let us, then, with courage and confidence, pursue our own federal and republican principles....our attachment to union and representative government. Kindly separated, by nature and a wide ocean, from the exterminating havoc of one quarter of the globe....too high-minded to endure the degradations of the others....possessing a chosen country, with room enough for our descendents to the thousandth and thousandth generation....entertaining a due sense of our equal right to the use of our own faculties....to the acquisitions of our own industry....to honour and confidence from our fellow-citizens; resulting not from birth, but from our actions, and their sense of them....enlightened by a benign religion, professed, indeed, and practised in various forms, yet all of them inculcating honesty, truth, temperance, gratitude, and the love of man....acknowledging and adoring an over-ruling Providence, which, by all its dispensations, proves that it delights in the happiness of man here, and his greater happiness hereafter....with all these blessings, what more is necessary to make us a happy and a prosperous people?....Still one thing more, fellow-citizens, a wise and frugal government, which shall restrain men from injuring one another; shall leave them otherwise free to regulate their own pursuits of industry and improvement; and shall not take from the mouth of labor the bread it has earned. This is the sum of good government; and this is necessary to close the circle of our felicities.

About to enter, fellow-citizens, on the exercise of duties, which comprehend every thing dear and valuable to you, it is proper you should understand what I deem the essential principles of our government, and consequently those which ought to shape its administration. I will compress them within the narrowest compass they will bear, stating the general principle, but not all its limitations. Equal and exact justice to all men, of whatever state or persuasion, religious or political....peace, commerce, and honest friendship with all nations....entangling alliances with none....the support of the state governments in all their rights, as the most competent administrations for our domestic concerns, and the surest bulwarks against anti-republican tendencies....the preservation of the general

government in its whole constitutional vigor, as the sheet anchor of our peace at home, and safety abroad....a jealous care of the right of election by the people....a mild and safe corrective of abuses, which are lopped by the sword of revolution, where peaceable remedies are unprovided.... absolute acquiescence in the decisions of the majority, the vital principle of republics, from which is no appeal but to force, the vital principle and immediate parent of despotism....a well-disciplined militia, our best reliance in peace, and for the first moments of war, till regulars may relieve them....the supremacy of the civil over the military authority....economy in the public expence, that labor may be lightly burdened....the honest payment of our debts, and sacred preservation of public faith....encouragement of agriculture, and of commerce, as its handmaid....the diffusion of information, and arraignment of all abuses at the bar of the public reason....freedom of religion....freedom of the press....and freedom of person, under the protection of the habeas corpus, and trial by juries impartially selected. These principles form the bright constellation, which has gone before us, and guided our steps through an age of revolution and reformation. The wisdom of our sages, and blood of our heroes, have been devoted, to their attainment. They should be the creed of our political faith....the text of civic instruction....the touchstone by which to try the services of those we trust: and should we wander from them, in moments of error or alarm, let us hasten to retrace our steps, and to regain the road which alone leads to peace, liberty, and safety.

I repair, then, fellow citizens, to the post you have assigned me. With experience enough in subordinate offices, to have seen the difficulties of this, the greatest of all, I have learned to expect, that it will rarely fall to the lot of imperfect man, to retire from this station, with the reputation, and the favor, which bring him into it. Without pretensions to that high confidence you reposed in our first and greatest revolutionary character, whose pre-eminent services had entitled him to the first place in his country's love, and destined for him the fairest page in the volume of faithful history, I ask so much confidence only, as may give firmness and effect to the legal administration of your affairs. I shall often go wrong, through defect of judgment. When right, I shall often be thought wrong, by those whose positions will not command a view of the whole ground. I ask your indulgence for my own errors, which will never be intentional; and your support against the errors of others, who may condemn what they would not, if seen in all its parts. The approbation implied by your suffrage, is a great consolation to me for the past: and my future solicitude will be, to retain the good opinion of those who have bestowed it in advance, to conciliate that of others by doing them all the good in my power, and to be instrumental to the happiness and freedom of all.

Relying, then, on the patronage of your good will, I advance with obedience to the work, ready to retire from it whenever you become sensible how much better choices it is in your power to make. And may that infinite Power, which rules the destinies of the universe, lead our councils to what is best, and give them a favourable issue, for our peace and prosperity.

THOMAS JEFFERSON.

THIRD EDITION.

PHILADELPHIA, PUBLISHED BY MATHEW CAREY.

H. MAXWELL, PRINTER.

Broadside of Jefferson's first inaugural address, March 4, 1801, published by Matthew Carey, Philadelphia, 1801. Engraving by Benjamin Tanner. (Courtesy of the Massachusetts Historical Society)

Replying to Monroe on May 29, Jefferson made the case for more open communications between federal officials and the governors of the states. He explained, "I think the practice in Genl. Washington's administration was most friendly to business and was absolutely equal. Sometimes he wrote to the governors, and sometimes the heads of departments wrote. If a letter is to be on a general subject, I see no reason why the President should not write: but if it is to go into details, these being known only to the head of the department, it is better he should write directly …. On the whole I think a free correspondence best and shall never hesitate to write myself to the governors."[71] Monroe accepted Jefferson's position, and their difference did not affect their continuing friendship and cooperation.

Meanwhile, Jefferson was occupied with getting his new administration underway. "We are hunting out and abolishing multitudes of useless offices, striking off jobs, etc., etc.," Jefferson wrote to his son-in-law, Thomas Mann Randolph, Jr. "Never were such scenes of favoritism, dissipation of treasure, and disregard of legal appropriation seen."[72] To Monroe, Jefferson wrote about the expenses of government under the previous Adams administration and confided, "These are things of the existence of which no man dreamt, and we are lopping them down silently to make as little noise as possible. They have been covered from the public under the head of contingencies, quartermaster's department, etc."[73]

From Richmond, on June 20, 1801, Governor Monroe wrote to President Jefferson in Washington, inquiring when he expected to be at Monticello. Hoping to see Jefferson in Albemarle County while he was there, Monroe added, "The season begins to approach when it becomes dangerous for those accustomed to a better climate to stay here," referring to the common practice of leaving Washington and other eastern cities in the late summer to avoid diseases such as yellow fever.[74] Soon after writing this letter, Monroe left for Albemarle County, where James Madison wrote to him, "hearing that you are with Mrs. Monroe in Albemarle."[75]

On July 4, Jefferson hosted a celebration at the President's House. He did not leave Washington until July 30, arriving at Monticello on August 2. From there Jefferson administered the duties of the presidential office, conferred with Monroe, and attended to his own affairs at Monticello until September 27, when he departed to return to Washington.

Washington City, 1821, *by Baroness Hyde de Neuville, wife of the French minister to the United States. (Courtesy of the Rare Books and Manuscripts Division, The New York Public Library, I. N. Stokes Collection)*

When the first session of the Seventh Congress met on December 7, 1801, Jefferson did not deliver his address in person, as the two previous presidents had done. Instead, convinced that the annual deliverance of a speech by the president resembled monarchical practices, Jefferson sent his message to be read to Congress by a clerk.

When Monroe read a copy of Jefferson's address, he wrote to him, "Your last communication to the Congress has placed your administration on such ground with the republican party, as to leave it in your power to act with respect to removals from office, as you may judge expedient.... It may also be said that it has produced such an effect among the people generally, as to put it in your power, especially if the taxes named be repealed without the danger of future recurrence to them, to remove whomsoever you think of the dependants of the late Administration are entitled to that mark of attention."[76] Monroe continued to give encouragement to the president in support of the changes underway, writing in April 1802, "the mild republican course of your administration has tended to put at repose the republicans and relieve from further apprehension the federalists."[77]

Soon after Monroe's third term as governor of Virginia ended in December 1802, President Jefferson had a major new assignment for him. In haste he wrote to Monroe on January 10, 1803:

I have but a moment to inform you that the fever into which the western mind is thrown by the affair at N. Orleans stimulated by the mercantile, and generally the federal interest threatens to overbear our peace. In this situation we are obliged to call on you for a temporary sacrifice of yourself, to prevent this greatest of evils in the present prosperous tide of our affairs. I shall tomorrow nominate you to the Senate for an extraordinary mission to France, and the circumstances are such as to render it impossible to decline; because the whole public hope will be rested on you. I wish you to be either in Richmond or Albemarle till you receive another letter from me, which will be written two days hence if the Senate decide immediately or later according to the time they will take to decide. In the meantime pray work night and day to arrange your affairs for a temporary absence; perhaps for a long one.[78]

The affair of New Orleans that brought this summons to Monroe had been brewing since rumors of the transfer of Louisiana from Spain to France had circulated in the United States. In April 1802, Jefferson had written to Robert R. Livingston, the United States minister to France, instructing him to impress upon the French government the inevitable consequences of their taking possession of Louisiana. That day would seal the union between the United States and Great Britain. "From that moment we must marry ourselves to the British fleet and nation. We must turn all our attention to a maritime force."[79]

In his instructions to Monroe, Jefferson stressed, "on the event of this mission depend the future destinies of this republic. If we cannot by a purchase of the country, insure to ourselves a course of perpetual peace and friendship with all nations, then as war cannot be distant, it behooves us immediately to be preparing for that course, without, however, hastening it."[80] Monroe was authorized to pay up to fifty million livres—slightly more than nine million dollars—for New Orleans and the Floridas.

Monroe, his wife, and their two daughters left New York on March 8 and reached Paris on April 12. Meanwhile, Robert R. Livingston had been negotiating without success for a purchase. On April 11, while the Monroes were en route from Le Havre to Paris, French minister Talleyrand suddenly summoned Livingston to a conference and startled him by asking if the United States would be interested in purchasing all of Louisiana.[81]

With Monroe's arrival in Paris, negotiations accelerated, and by the end of the month Monroe and Livingston had negotiated the treaty for the purchase of Louisiana for fifteen million dollars. The treaty was signed on May 2, 1803. The news of the treaty reached Washington on July 3, in time for the signing of the treaty to be announced in the Washington *National Intelligencer* on the Fourth of July.

After the signing of the treaty for the Louisiana Purchase, Monroe carried out diplomatic missions to London and Madrid before returning to the United States in December 1807. He was in London when the British ship *Leopard* fired on the United States frigate *Chesapeake* off the Virginia capes on June 22, 1807. Monroe and William Pinkney were charged with negotiating a treaty with the British, with the chief and possibly over-optimistic aim of ending the British practice of "impressing" sailors from American ships into service on British ships. The sailors drafted into duty were presumably British deserters but in fact were often American citizens. When the British refused to yield on the issue, Monroe and Pinkney negotiated a treaty that sidestepped the question. President Jefferson was so displeased with the treaty that he did not submit it to the Senate for ratification.

Monroe's failure to negotiate a successful treaty threatened their friendship for a time. Jefferson offered Monroe the post of governor of the Louisiana territory whenever Monroe returned to the United States, but Monroe did not accept.[82] Later Jefferson wrote to ask Monroe to make a purchase for him in London, adding, "I had intended to have written you to counteract the wicked efforts which the federal papers are making to sow tares between you and me." He assured Monroe, "I shall receive you on your return with the warm affection I have ever entertained for you, and be gratified if I can in any way avail the public of your services."[83]

Monroe, his wife, and two daughters arrived in Norfolk on December 13, 1807, after having been absent from the United States for nearly four years. When they returned, the approaching presidential election of 1808 was already dominating political life. In Virginia, James Madison, Jefferson's secretary of state and longtime friend, was well positioned to become the Republican presidential candidate. Madison was the senior candidate in government service, but Monroe also had the national standing and the friendship of Jefferson to attract wide support as a candidate for president. His experience as minister to France in the 1790s and his diplomatic success in Paris in the purchase of Louisiana during Jefferson's first term as president made Monroe an attractive contender. On January 21, the friends of Madison and the friends of Monroe held competing nominating caucuses in Richmond and nominated their respective candidates.

As the contest for the presidency between Madison and Monroe loomed larger, Jefferson wrote to Monroe early in 1808:

> I see with infinite grief a contest arising between yourself and another, who have been very dear to each other, and equally so to me. I sincerely pray that these dispositions may not be affected between you; with me I confidently trust they will not. For independently of the dictates of public duty, which prescribe neutrality to me, my sincere friendship for you both will ensure it's sacred observance. I suffer no one to converse with me on the subject.... The object of the contest is a fair and honorable one, equally open to you all; and I have no doubt the personal conduct of all will be so chaste, as to offer no ground of dissatisfaction with each other.... I have ever viewed Mr. Madison and yourself as two principal pillars of my happiness. Were either to be withdrawn, I should consider it as among the greatest calamities which could assail my future peace of mind.[84]

As a backdrop to the continuing difficulties in Monroe and Jefferson's relationship, Monroe continued to seethe over lasting repercussions of the failure of the treaty that he—with the unwelcome assistance of William Pinkney—had negotiated with the British concerning the issue of impressment. In a long letter to the president written from Richmond on February 17, 1808, Monroe poured out his feelings: "I can assure you that no occurrences of my whole life ever gave me so much concern as some which took place during my absence abroad, proceeding from the present administration. I allude more especially to the mission of Mr. Pinkney with all the circumstances connected with that measure, and the manner in which the treaty which he and I formed, which was in fact little more than a project, was received…. When I returned to the U States I found that heavy censure had fallen on me in the publick opinion, as I had before much reason to believe was the case, in consequence of my having signed the British treaty."[85]

Monroe went on to argue that when he returned to Richmond, he was assured that his action had been used against him "with great effect in relation to a particular object," by which he meant a candidacy for the presidency of the United States.[86] In a long letter in response, Jefferson assured

Thomas Jefferson *by Gilbert Stuart, 1805. (Owned jointly by the National Portrait Gallery, Smithsonian Institution, and the Thomas Jefferson Foundation, Inc., Monticello. Gift of Regents of the Smithsonian, Thomas Jefferson Foundation, Inc., and Enid and Crosby Kemper Foundation)*

Monroe, "If you have been made to believe that I ever did, said, or thought a thing unfriendly to your fame and feelings, you do me injury as causeless as it is afflicting to me. In the present contest in which you are concerned, I feel no passion, I take no part, I express no sentiment. Whichever of my friends is called to the supreme cares of the nation, I know they will be wisely and faithfully administered, and as far as my individual conduct can influence, they shall be cordially supported."[87]

When the congressional nominating caucus named James Madison as the candidate for president to succeed Jefferson, support for Monroe faded. Madison won a decisive victory with Monroe receiving three votes for vice president but no votes for president. As Jefferson's presidential term drew to a close, in late January 1809 Monroe proposed that before leaving office, Jefferson send him on another mission to France and England. In a long letter, Monroe wrote, "Our affairs are evidently at a pause, and the next step ... seems likely to be the commencement of a war with both France & England. It is all important to avoid such a result if possible, and in case it is not, that we should enter into the war with the greatest union of which our system is capable. It has occurred that before that step is taken, some signal effort should be resorted to for that purpose.... I am willing to undertake this trust and set out in discharge of it without a moment's delay, leaving my family behind. From my acquaintance with both governments, I should undertake it with strong hope of success."[88]

In response, Jefferson wrote frankly, "The idea of sending a special mission to France or England is not entertained at all here.... The idea was hazarded in the House of Representatives a few days ago, by a member, and an approbation expressed by another, but rejected indignantly by every other person who spoke, and very generally in conversation by all others; and I am satisfied such a proposition would get no vote in the Senate." The president closed his letter by writing, "Five weeks more will relieve me from the drudgery to which I am no longer equal, and restore me to a scene of tranquillity, amidst my family and friends, more congenial to my age and natural inclinations. In that situation, it will always be a pleasure to me to see you, and to repeat to you the assurances of my constant friendship and respect."[89]

Chapter Three

1809-1815

James Madison was inaugurated as the fourth president of the United States on March 4, 1809. Although James Monroe had posed a challenge to Madison's election, the new president did not break relations with his old friend. President Madison, initially, however, did not invite Monroe to join his cabinet. In a letter to Madison at the end of March, Jefferson wrote: "Colo. Monroe dined and passed an evening with me since I came home. He is sincerely cordial.... I did not enter into any material political conversation with him, and still less as to the present course of things because I shall have better opportunities on his return with his family." Jefferson noted that Monroe had recently separated himself from an acrimonious political clique: "On the whole I have no doubt that his strong and candid mind will bring to a cordial return to his old friends after he shall have been separated a while from his present circle, which separation I think is one of the objects of his removal from Richmond, with which place he expressed to me much disgust."[90] In November 1809, Madison asked Jefferson to sound out Monroe about accepting the governorship of Louisiana, but Monroe refused to consider any post in which he would be subordinate to anyone except the president.[91]

The strained relations between Jefferson and Monroe lessened when, in late February 1810, Jefferson made a call on Monroe, who was ill.[92] In April 1810, Monroe returned to active political life with his election to the Virginia Assembly. After Virginia Governor John Tyler resigned to accept a federal judgeship, Monroe once more was elected governor in January 1811. Three months later, President Madison invited Monroe to join his cabinet as secretary of state, and Monroe did not hesitate to accept the appointment.[93] After Monroe returned to Washington, Jefferson wrote to him from Monticello in May 1811: "Although I may not have been among the first, I am certainly with the sincerest, who congratulate you on your entrance into the national councils. Your value there has never been unduly estimated by those whom personal feelings did not misguide."[94]

A year later, the declaration of war by the United States against Great Britain on June 19, 1812, placed heavy burdens on Jefferson's two closest friends: Madison and Monroe.[95] As secretary of state, Monroe kept the now-retired Jefferson well informed on foreign affairs, though the pressures of the war of 1812 often delayed his reports. In early June 1813, Monroe began a long letter to Jefferson: "During the last session of Congress the current business pressed so heavily on me, and after its adjournment, the preparation of instructions for our Ministers employed under the mediation of Russia, and in other duties connected with it, kept me so constantly engaged that I have scarcely had a moment of respite since I left you. I seize one to communicate some details, which it may be satisfactory for you to know. As I make the communication in confidence, it will be without reserve."[96] This detailed letter filled thirteen pages on seven sheets of paper.[97] When Monroe closed it, he asked Jefferson to return the letter, "it being the only copy which I have."[98]

Meanwhile on May 30, Jefferson had written to Monroe proposing "the policy of keeping our frigates together in a body, in some place where they can be defended against a superior naval force, and from whence, nevertheless, they can easily sally forth on the shortest warning. This would oblige the enemy to take stations, or to cruise only in masses equal at least, each of them, to our whole force; and of course they could be acting only in two or three spots at a time, and the whole of our coast, except the two or three portions where they might be present, would be open to exportation and importation."[99] After reading this letter, Monroe responded, "The reasoning against it, in which all our naval officers have agreed, is that if stationed together, in a port, New York for example, the British would immediately block it up thus, by a force rather superior, and then harrass our coast and commerce without restraint, and with any force however small."[100] In reply, thanking Monroe for his kind answer, Jefferson wrote that it "shows how erroneous views are apt to be with those who have not all in view."[101]

While Jefferson refrained from further military advice, he followed the course of the war as closely as information available to him permitted, typical of his retirement behavior. After the burning of Washington by the British on August 24, 1814, Jefferson waited a month before writing to Monroe. He began his letter by noting, "The events which have lately taken place at Washington, and which truly disgrace our enemies much more than us, have occupied you too much to admit intrusions by private and useless letters." Following comments on the state of the nation, Jefferson closed, "Having learnt by the public papers the loss of the library of Congress, I have sent my catalogue to S. H. Smith with an offer of the whole collection, as it stands, to the library committee, to be valued by persons named by themselves, delivered immediately and paid for in such stock, or otherwise, and at such epoch as they may chuse after the days of peace and prosperity shall have returned. You know the general condition of the books, and can give them information should they ask any."[102]

When Monroe received Jefferson's letter, he wrote immediately to him from Washington: "Nothing but the disasters here, and the duties which have devolved on me in consequence, the most burthensome that I have ever encountered, would have prevented my writing you long since, as well as more recently."[103] Still pressed with duties, Monroe delayed answering Jefferson's letter immediately, but he did so a few days later, assuring Jefferson: "I shall be happy to promote the disposition

Capitol, sketch after 1812 burning (courtesy of the Historical Society of Washington, D.C.; gift of James Goode)

of your library in the manner you propose, tho' I regret that you are deprived of such a resource and consolation in your retirement."[104]

After the burning of Washington by the British, Monroe was so occupied with his duties that it was late December before he found time to write a long, reflective letter to Jefferson explaining how he had come "not as a volunteer" to serve temporarily as secretary of war following the attack of the capital. He shared his opinion that the "city might have been saved, had the measures proposed by the President… been carried into effect," but that General Armstrong "could never be made to believe that it was in any danger." Following the dismissal of War Secretary William Eustis, President Madison requested Monroe to add for a time the duties of secretary of war to his current responsibilities as secretary of state. "The pressure on Alexandria and approaching attack on Baltimore with other dangers and in many quarters allowed not a moment of respite for the department. 24 hours of inaction was sure to produce serious mischief. These considerations induced me to retain the office & to incur a labour, & expose myself to a responsibility, the nature & extent of which I well understood, & whose weight has already almost borne me down." He continued with an assessment about the "deplorable" finances of the union: "With a country consisting of the best materials in the world, whose people are patriotic & virtuous, & willing to support the war; whose resources are greater than those of any other country; & whose means have scarcely yet been touched, we have neither treasury or credit."[105]

Jefferson replied with his own perspective on the "embarrassments at Washington," noting that "Nearly every Capital [in Europe] was in possession of its enemy; some often and long." But the burning of the public and private buildings of the American capital, continued Jefferson, was a means "for England to show that Bonaparte, in atrocity, was an infant to their ministers and their generals. They are taking his place in the eyes of Europe, and have turned into our channel all its good will. This will be worth the million of dollars the repairs of their conflagration will cost us." As to Monroe's new responsibilities, Jefferson added, "I much regretted your acceptance of the war department. Not that I know a person who I think would better conduct it. But, conduct it ever so wisely, it will be a sacrifice of yourself. Were an angel from Heaven to undertake that office, all our miscarriages would be ascribed to him.... Not that I have seen the least disposition to censure you. On the contrary, your conduct on the attack of Washington has met with the praises of every one."[106]

At the time they exchanged these letters, it was unknown to either Jefferson or Monroe that a peace treaty had been signed in Ghent on December 24, 1814. Nor could they know that a major battle being fought in New Orleans would bring the greatest American land victory of the war two weeks after the signing of the peace treaty at Ghent.

On February 15, 1815, Monroe wrote to Jefferson from Washington, "It is with infinite satisfaction that I inform you of the arrival of Mr. [Henry] Carroll yesterday from Ghent, with a treaty of peace between the UStates and G. Britain which was concluded on the 24 of Dec. last. It is in all respects honorable to our country. No concession is made of any kind.... It is evident that this treaty has been extorted from the British ministry. The late victory at New Orleans terminates this contest with peculiar advantage and even splendour to the UStates. The treaty will be submitted to the Senate today and I presume approved without opposition.[107]

As the presidential election year of 1816 began, Jefferson wrote to Monroe in February, "It is impossible for you to note and preserve every thing as it passes in newspapers. I have therefore cut out of the Virginia Argus of Feb. 14 the enclosed paper. Have it filed with the papers on the Louisiana title, and when you have to take up that subject it will suggest to you facts for enquiry." Though retired, Jefferson continued to offer Monroe assistance, whether as a news-clipping service, or a sounding board for ideas and issues.[108]

Detail from The Old House of Representatives *by Samuel Finley Breese Morse, 1822. (Courtesy of the Corcoran Gallery of Art, Museum Purchase, Gallery Fund)*

Chapter Four

1816-1820

On the evening of March 16, 1816, the Republican congressional nominating caucus, meeting in the House chamber, nominated James Monroe as the Republican candidate for president of the United States. When no Federalist caucus nominated a candidate to oppose Monroe and no Federalist actively challenged his election, Monroe won all but three states. On March 4, 1817, Monroe was inaugurated as the fifth president of the United States.

Before the electoral votes had been officially counted, Jefferson was making recommendations to Monroe regarding the task of restoring the public buildings burned by the British during the War of 1812. If any inscription were to be placed on the restored Capitol, he suggested the following be inscribed within a triangle:

FOUNDED 1791

BURNED BY A BRITISH ARMY 1814

RESTORED BY CONGRESS 1817

"The reasons for this brevity are that the letters must be of extraordinary magnitude to be read from below," he wrote. He then went on to add, "But a question of more importance is whether there should be one at all? The barbarism of the conflagration will immortalise that of the nation. It will place them for ever in degraded comparison with the execrated Bonaparte who, in possession of almost every capital in Europe, injured no one. Of this, history will take care, which all will read, while our inscription will be seen by few."[109] Jefferson's proposal was never implemented.

Monroe's election to the presidency in 1816 prompted the artist Jonathan Trumbull to ask Jefferson to recommend his services to the new president. In response to the request, Jefferson wrote to Monroe,

> It would seem mighty idle for me to inform you formally of the merits of Col. Trumbull as a painter or as a man. Yet he asks my notice of him to my friends, as if his talents had not already distinguished him in their notice. On the continent of Europe his genius was placed much above West's…. Col. Trumbull expects that as the legislature are with liberality rebuilding the public edifices, they will proceed in the same spirit to their decoration. If so, his paintings should certainly be their first object. They will be monuments of the taste and talents of our country, as well as of the scenes which gave it its place among nations. I recommend him to your kind offices, and rejoice in seeing that you are to be in a place where they may have effect.[110]

Little more than a week before taking office as president, Monroe responded to Jefferson's recent letters. Regarding Jefferson's recommendation of Trumbull, he wrote, "I had the pleasure to receive the letter which you forwarded to me through Col. Trumbull, & to apply it, with the best effect, to the purpose for which it was intended. Congress passed a law … for the painting of four pieces; the Declaration of Independence, the Surrender of Burgoyne, that of Cornwallis, & the resignation of Genl. Washington…. I am satisfied that he owes this tribute of respect, principally, to your favorable opinion of his merit."

The president-elect also explained his decision to name John Quincy Adams—and not a Virginian—to be head of the state department: "You know how much has been said to impress a belief, on the country, north & east of this, that the citizens of Virginia, holding the Presidency, have made appointments to that department, to secure the succession, from it, to the Presidency, of the person who happens to be from that State…. It is not sufficient that this allegation is unfounded…. With this in view, I have thought it advisable to select a person for the department of State, from the Eastern states, in consequence of which my attention has been turned to Mr. Adams, who by his age, long experience in our foreign affairs, and adoption into the republican party, seems to have superior pretentions to any there."[111]

Jefferson was not in Washington for the inauguration of Monroe as president of the United States on March 4, 1817. Monroe's long address offered few memorable passages to evoke later commentary. When Jefferson addressed a letter to Monroe on April 8, he began, "I shall not waste your time in idle congratulations. You know my joy on the commitment of the helm of our government to your hands." Perhaps tactfully, Jefferson did not comment on Monroe's inaugural

James Monroe, President of the United States. *Engraved print by Thomas Gimbrede, 1817. (Courtesy of the James Monroe Museum and Memorial Library)*

address, although he included a detailed commentary on wines he had ordered from France.[112] Jefferson's attention at that time, however, focused on more pressing matters than wines. A few days later, he wrote to Monroe reporting on plans to create a college "at your former residence above Charlottesville":

> The receipt of a commission as Visitor will have informed you, if you did not know it before, that we have in contemplation to establish a College near Charlottesville…. [I]t is to be under the direction of 6 visitors. Your commission has informed you you were one of these…. A meeting, and immediately, is indispensable to fix the site, purchase the grounds, begin building, etc…. The legislature at their next meeting will locate the University they propose, on a truly great scale, and with ample funds…. The centrality of Charlottesville and other favorable circumstances places it on the highest ground of competition…. The commencement of the buildings immediately will draw the public attention to it, but what everyone believes will bring

it the most notice is a full meeting of the Visitors. The attendance of yourself there, Mr. Madison and others will be a spectacle which will vividly strike the public eye, will be talked of, put onto the papers, coupled with the purpose, and give preeminence to the place.... It will silence cis-montane competition, unite suffrages, and insure us against schism. Your attendance *for this once* is looked for with great desire ... by the people of this section of country, and you can never do an act so gratifying to them, as by joining this meeting. As a visit to your farm however short must be desirable to you, I am in hopes you will so time it as to meet us on the occasion.[113]

Monroe replied, "It would give me sincere pleasure, to attend the meeting of visitors to be held on the 5th of May, for establishing the site of the central college, in our county, and I will do it, if in my power.... There are no very important duties, pressing here, at this time, but you well know, that there never is a moment, in which there is not some thing of interest, and often of an embarrassing kind.... For the interest you take in my success, which is always very gratifying and consoling to me, I am truly thankful."[114]

When the Board of Visitors convened their first regular meeting on May 5, 1817, President Monroe was present along with former presidents Jefferson and Madison. The board speedily approved Jefferson's plan for an academical village and authorized the beginning of construction of the college that would become the University of Virginia. A few weeks later, ex-president John Adams wrote to Jefferson, "I congratulate you and Madison and Monroe, on your noble Employment in founding a University. From such a noble Tryumvirate, the World will expect something very great and very new."[115]

While Jefferson worked to get construction under way, Monroe departed Washington on May 31, beginning an extended tour that in three and a half months carried the president through thirteen states. After two months of travel, on July 27, 1817, Monroe wrote to Jefferson from Plattsburg, New York: "I have been exposed to excessive fatigue & labor, in my tour, by the pressure of a very crowded population, which has sought to manifest its respect, for our Union, &

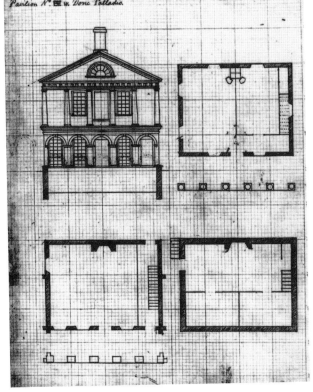

Letter from Thomas Jefferson to William Thornton, May 9, 1817 including a sketch of an early plan for the Lawn at the University of Virginia. (Courtesy of Special Collections, University of Virginia Library)

Study by Thomas Jefferson for Pavilion VII, July 1817. This pavilion was the first building constructed at the University of Virginia. (Courtesy of Special Collections, University of Virginia Library) republican institutions.... I have seen enough to satisfy me, that the great mass of our fellow-citizens, in the Eastern States are as firmly attached to the union and to the republican government as I have always believed or could desire them to be." More personally, he wrote, "I hope to see you the latter end of next month, when we will enter into the details, which the few minutes I now enjoy do not admit, however glad I should be to do it. I most ardently wish to get home, to meet my family & friends & to enjoy in peace some moments of repose to which I have been an utter stranger since I left Washington."[116]

While Monroe was traveling, Jefferson pressed forward with his plans for a university in Virginia. When he sent Monroe a copy of a letter relating to its location, Monroe responded with his endorsement: "I had nothing to alter in, or add to it. I hope and think, that it will succeed, in placing the University, where it ought to be; and that, by means of that institution, the character of the State, for distinguished merited acquirement, in its citizens, will be maintained, in the high rank, it has heretofore sustained."[117]

When President Monroe was at Highland, his home near Jefferson in Albemarle County, he stayed in close touch with Jefferson. In a note to Jefferson in October 1818, he wrote, "J. Monroe has the pleasure to submit to Mr. Jefferson's perusal a letter from Judge Bland, on South American affairs, which he mentioned to him sometime since. If the weather and Mr. Jefferson's health permit, J. M. will be very much gratified by his company today, with the gentlemen, now at Monticello, who promised, with Col. Randolph, to dine with him today."[118]

Monroe regularly kept Jefferson informed of what was happening in Washington, and in January 1819, Jefferson wrote to him. "You oblige me infinitely, dear Sir, by sending me the Congressional documents in pamphlet form. For as they come out piece-meal in the newspapers I never read them.... But in a pamphlet, where we can go thro' the whole subject when once taken up, and seen in all it's parts, we avoid the risk of false judgment which a partial view endangers."[119]

On February 22, 1819, the United States acquired Florida under the treaty negotiated by Secretary of State John Quincy Adams and the Spanish minister to the United States, Luis de Onís. The treaty also settled to Spain's satisfaction the border of Texas and for the first time in official annals set the western boundary

James Monroe *by John Vanderlyn, 1822. (Courtesy of the Art Commission of the City of New York, from the collections of the City of New York)*

of the United States at the Pacific Ocean. The Senate approved the treaty on February 24, 1819.[120]

In February 1820, Monroe wrote to Jefferson, "I send you by this days mail, the documents of greatest interest, which have been presented to Congress during the present Session. On our concerns with Spain we have nothing new, and little reason to expect a Minister here from that country, during the Session.... The Missouri question, absorbs by its importance, and the excit'ment it has produc'd, every other and there is little prospect, from present appearances of its being soon settled."[121]

At the time Monroe wrote this letter, the Missouri question had become far more than the issue of admitting a new state. "I have never known a question so menacing to the tranquility and even the continuance of our Union as the present one," Monroe wrote to Jefferson on February 19, 1820.[122] Not long afterward, Jefferson wrote similarly to Monroe: "This Missouri question by a geographical line of division is the most portentous one I have ever contemplated."[123]

The critical question was whether Missouri should be admitted as a slave state. After a long and divisive debate in Congress, the famous compromise was reached. Missouri and Maine (which had also applied for statehood) were admitted without any restriction, and slavery was excluded in any future states located north of 36°30'. [124]

Pondering the outcome of the Missouri controversy and the growing issue of slavery, Jefferson at Monticello wrote, "this momentous question, like a fire bell in the night, awakened and filled me with terror. I considered it at once as the knell of the Union. It is hushed, indeed, for the moment. But this is a reprieve only, not a final sentence."[125] Thanking President Monroe for a letter received in May 1820, Jefferson wrote, "These texts of truth relieve me from the floating falsehoods of the public press."[126]

Whenever Monroe was at his home near Jefferson's, he not only saw Jefferson frequently but also sent him various papers to read to keep the retired statesman abreast of current issues. From Highland during his summer recess in 1820, President Monroe wrote, "In addition to Mr. Gallatin's and Mr. Rush's letters which I promised last night to send you today, I enclose a copy of the instructions given to Mr. Forbes, appointed agent to So. America, either Buenos Ayres or Chili, to be decided, by a circumstance mentioned in them. As they explain in a general way, our relations with that country, and state some facts of an interesting nature I have thought that it might be agreeable to you to see them."[127]

James Monroe L.L.D. President of the United States. *Engraving by Charles Goodman and Robert Piggott after painting by Charles Bird King. Published by William H. Morgan. Philadelphia, 1817. (Courtesy of the Library of Congress)*

Chapter Five

1821-1826

On March 5, 1821, James Monroe took the oath of office as president of the United States for a second term, following a presidential election in which only one electoral vote was cast against him. Throughout his second term, Monroe continued to correspond regularly with the retired and aging Jefferson, keeping him informed on national affairs and soliciting his advice.

In the summer of 1821, Jefferson received a letter from officials in Poland regarding plans to erect a monument in memory of Thaddeus Kosciuszko, the Polish general who had fought on the American side against Great Britain during the American Revolution. In August, Jefferson wrote to Monroe:

> You have seen announced in several of our papers an intention of the Polonese nation to erect a monument near Cracow to the memory of Genl. Kosciuzko, and their wish that England and the U.S. by joining in contributions might give a proof of the interest they take in his character.... I received in fact such a letter some weeks ago from the President of the Senate of Cracow, with an indication that it should be communicated to you also. Much at a loss to devise in what way I could set about the execution of this proposition, I have held the subject for some time under consideration. Retired as I am, among the mountains of our interior country, I see nobody but the farmers of my neighborhood who would consider contributions to public monuments in other countries as very foreign to the condition and business of their lives.

Jefferson continued with his thoughts on the subject and asked Monroe to take on the issue, noting that "the heavy hand of age …[has] rendered me quite unequal to the correspondence it might require, and unfit to become the center of such an operation."[128]

In reply to Jefferson, Monroe agreed to undertake to relieve Jefferson of the projected burden and "to evince my profound respect for the character of General Kosciusko," but he was doubtful of success. It was natural for the Polish nation to look to the United States for support. "But the great demand which has been and is still made on them, in various ways, in support of institutions and measures on which their highest interests depend, has been so sensibly felt that a like attempt in honor of the memory of General Washington has recently failed in this State, nor has a statue yet been erected to his memory by the nation."[129]

After Jefferson broke his arm in November 1822, Monroe wrote to him to express his concern:

> We have all been very much distressed, at the accounts recently received, of the misfortune you have sustained, in the fracture of your arm, or at least of one of its bones. We hope that it has not been so serious, as had been represented, and that you are rapidly recovering from it.
>
> This is a moment, as you well know, when, in addition to the heavy cases which bear on me, the calls of the members of Congress, which cannot be resisted, and of others, absorb my whole time; tho' in truth I have little interesting to communicate to you. The inclosed letter will give the most recent and authentic accounts from Mexico. They are however of a distressing character. Return it to me under a blank cover after perusing it.[130]

Jefferson's broken arm was still troubling him when he wrote to William Short in March 1823, and he sent Monroe a copy of this letter. Short, who had been Jefferson's private secretary when Jefferson was the United States minister to France, was planning to visit Jefferson in the autumn. In his letter to Short,

Jefferson proudly reported, "Our University is now compleat to a single building, which, having seen the Pantheon, your imagination will readily supply, so as to form a good idea of its ultimate appearance. You must bequeath it your library, as many others of us propose to do."[131]

The broad extent to which President Monroe kept Jefferson informed about international affairs is demonstrated by the following letter, written from Washington, June 2, 1823. The letter also well illustrates the mature Monroe at the height of his presidency. Monroe expressed his regret at missing Jefferson during his last visit to Albemarle County, but explained that he "was compelled to return, to receive the instructions, which had just been prepared, for our ministers, who were just about to sail for Spain & So. America, & by other duties. The moment is peculiarly critical, as respects the present state of the world, & our relations with the acting parties in it, in Europe, & in this hemisphere, & it would have been very gratifying to me, to have had an opportunity of free communication with you, on all the interesting subjects connected with it." He summarized his understanding of the complex interrelationships of European countries, most particularly exploring the issue of French armies entering Spain to reinstate the authority of a restored monarch. The president asked Jefferson's opinion about whether the United States should take an active role in supporting republican principles in Europe, writing, "Can we, in any form, take a bolder attitude in regard to it, in favor of liberty, than we then did? Can we afford greater aid to that cause, by assuming any such attitude, than we now do, by our example? These are subjects on which I should be glad to have your sentiments." Turning to a subject dear to Jefferson's heart, he concluded, "I called at the University and was much gratified to find that the Rotunda had been commenced, and was in train of rapid execution. That the institution may be put in motion, as soon as possible, is an object of general solicitude."[132]

In reply, Jefferson noted the irony of his having been at his residence Poplar Forest in Bedford County while Monroe was in Albemarle: "Considering that I had not been to Bedford for a twelvemonth before, I thought myself singularly unfortunate in so timing my journey, as to have been absent exactly at the moment of your late visit to our neighborhood. The loss, indeed, was all my own; for in these short interviews with you, I generally get my political compass rectified, learn from you whereabouts we are, and correct my course again. In exchange for this, I can give you but newspaper ideas, and indeed little of these.... I find Horace and Tacitus so much better writers than the champions of the gazettes, that I lay those down to take up these with great reluctance."

Responding to Monroe's question of whether the United States should take a "bolder attitude ... in favor of liberty" in its dealings with Europe, Jefferson wrote that the "presumption of dictating to an independent nation the form of its government, is so arrogant, so atrocious...." He continued, "I have ever deemed it fundamental for the United States never to take active part in the quarrels of Europe. Their political interests are entirely distinct from ours.... They are nations of eternal war. All their energies are expended in the destruction of the labor, property, and lives of their people. On our part, never had a people so favorable a chance of trying the opposite system, of peace and fraternity with mankind."[133]

The close relationship between President Monroe and former President Jefferson is well illustrated in the letters that passed between them relating to what would become known as the Monroe Doctrine. From Oakhill, his house nearer to Washington than his home in Albemarle County, Monroe wrote to Jefferson on October 17, 1823. The key issue at hand was the independence of the former Spanish colonies in Central and South America, whose status as nations was recognized by President Monroe in 1822. Monroe passed along to Jefferson a copy of a letter from British Foreign Secretary George Canning, stating that England's former allies, European powers known as the "Holy Alliance," held "designs ... against the Independence of South America & proposing a co-opera-tion, between Great Britian & the United States, in support of it." Monroe dis-cussed his thoughts on the subject, positing their shared view of the importance of refusing to "entangle ourselves, at all, in European politicks," yet wondering "if a case can exist in which a maxim may, & ought to be departed from, is not the present instance, precisely that case?" He argued, "My own impression is that we ought to meet the proposal of the British government & to make it known, that we would view ... an attack on the Colonies [by European powers] as an attack on ourselves." Asking Jefferson to share the letter and the quandary with Madison,

Monroe concluded, "I am sensible however of the extent & difficulty of the question & shall be happy to have yours, & Mr. Madison's opinions on it. I do not wish to trouble either of you with small objects, but the present one is vital, involving the high interests, for which we have so long & so faithfully, & harmoniously, contended together."[134]

In a long letter that filled nearly three large pages, Jefferson promptly responded on October 24, 1823, opening, "The question presented by the letters you have sent me, is the most momentous which has ever been offered to my contemplation since that of Independance." Almost immediately, he offered two principles: "Our first and fundamental maxim should be, never to entangle ourselves in the broils of Europe. Our second, never to suffer Europe to intermeddle with cis-Atlantic affairs." Unequivocally, Jefferson favored working with the British government: "By acceding to her proposition, we detach her from the bands [of European despotism], bring her mighty weight into the scale of free government,

First paragraphs from the draft of letter from Thomas Jefferson to James Monroe, October 24, 1823. (Courtesy of the Library of Congress, Thomas Jefferson Papers)

and emancipate a continent at one stroke.... Great Britain is the nation which can do us the most harm of any one, or all on earth; and with her on our side we need not fear the whole world." Jefferson noted, "Not that I would purchase even her amity at the price of taking part in her wars. But the war in which the present proposition might engage us... is not her war, but ours." He agreed with Canning that a union of Great Britain and the United States would prevent military action: "With Great Britain withdrawn from their scale and shifted into that of our two continents, all Europe combined would not undertake such a war." Jefferson also discussed related questions, such as the possibility of American expansion in South America, confessing, "I have ever looked on Cuba as the most interesting addition which could ever be made to our system of States." Jefferson recognized, however, that such an addition would only be made through war, and wrote, "I have no hesitation in abandoning my first wish [for Cuba]... and accepting its independence, with peace the friendship of England." In an ongoing recognition of the limits that his retirement placed on his political involvement, Jefferson concluded, "I have been so long weaned from political subjects, and have so long ceased to take any interest in them, that I am sensible I am not qualified to offer opinions on them worthy of any attention. But the question now proposed involves consequences so lasting, and effects so decisive of our future destinies, as to rekindle all the interest I have heretofore felt on such occasions, and to induce me to the hazard of opinions.... And praying you to accept it at only what it is worth, I add the assurance of my constant and affectionate friendship and respect." [135]

In his seventh annual message to Congress on December 2, 1823, President Monroe declared "as a principle in which the rights and interests of the United States are involved, that the American continents, by the free and independent condition which they have assumed and maintain, are henceforth not to be considered as subjects for future colonization by any European powers." [136] He explained: "With the existing colonies or dependencies of any European power we have not interfered and shall not interfere. But with the Governments who have declared their independence and maintained it, and whose independence we have, on great consideration and on just principles, acknowledged, we could not view any interposition for the purpose of oppressing them, or controlling in any other manner their destiny, by any European power in any other light than as the manifestation of an unfriendly disposition toward the United States."[137]

As long as Monroe remained in office as president, he regularly kept both former presidents Jefferson and Madison informed on national affairs, and, at times, he asked them to share this information with each other.[138]

In the summer of 1824, some estrangement between Jefferson and Monroe resulted from Monroe's failure to appoint Bernard Peyton as the postmaster of Richmond. Jefferson had urged Peyton's appointment as a personal favor, but unknown to Jefferson was the fact that Jefferson's son-in-law Thomas Mann Randolph also had sought the position. Under these difficult circumstances, Monroe appointed former Governor James P. Preston to fill the post.[139]

While the burdens of the presidency heavily engaged Monroe, Jefferson devoted his final years to the building of the University of Virginia. President

West Front of the Capitol of the United States *by Charles Burton, 1825. From* Tribute of Respect from the City of New York to General Lafayette, the Illustrious Friend of Civil Liberty. *(Courtesy of the New-York Historical Society, negative number 64417)*

Monroe had planned to be present at a dinner honoring the visiting Marquis de Lafayette on November 5, 1824, but he was unable to attend and would be deprived of witnessing the moving events of that day. In the dome room of the unfinished Rotunda of the university, Jefferson—seated between Lafayette and James Madison—raised his glass in a toast to Lafayette, and he later heard himself toasted as the "founder of the University of Virginia."[140] It was to be Jefferson's last appearance at a public dinner.

In March 1825, Monroe closed his second term as president of the United States. He left office deeply in debt, some of it accumulated over many years. A substantial portion of his debt, in fact, dated back to his diplomatic service in France. In June 1825, much to Jefferson's regret, Monroe sold all of his land and property in Albemarle County, Virginia.[141]

With both Jefferson and Monroe heavily in debt, many of the last letters exchanged between them related to their efforts to deal with these increasing burdens. In February 1826, Monroe wrote to Jefferson, "I had seen in a paper from Richmond, a notice of an application which you had made to the legislature, for permission to sell a large portion of your estate, by lottery, for the payment of your debts." Monroe continued, "I have been much concerned to find, that your devotion to the public service ... should have had so distressing an effect, on your large private fortune, and my regret is the greater, from the interest I take in what relates to your family as well as to yourself." Monroe pledged his support for the lottery and noted that he had communicated it to others "with a request, that they would promote the object."[142] On March 8, Jefferson replied: "To keep a Virginia estate together requires in the owner both skill, which I never had and attention, I could not have, and really when I reflect on all circumstances my wonder is that I should have been so long as 60 years in reaching the result to which I am now reduced. Still if [the lottery] succeeds I am safe."[143]

Jefferson would maintain possession of his beloved Monticello until his death. Although his family eventually surrendered the plantation to pay Jefferson's debts, his unfortunate financial situation would not overshadow his many years of distinguished public service. It was that record by which Jefferson would be remembered long after he took his last breath on July 4, 1826, the fiftieth anniversary of the signing of the Declaration of Independence. In one of the extraordinary happenings in the history of the United States, on that same day, in Quincy, Massachusetts, former President John Adams also died. Equally astounding, five years later, in New York City, James Monroe died on July 4, 1831.

During much of the first half-century of rising strength of the United States of America, Thomas Jefferson and James Monroe participated, at different times and in differing ways, in the building of the young nation. Jefferson, the senior of the two men, earned a memorable place in the nation's history as the principal author of the American Declaration of Independence and the third president of the United States. Monroe also won lasting recognition in the record of the young nation by his service on major diplomatic missions, including that of the purchase of Louisiana. As the fifth president of the United States, Monroe may best be known for articulating the premise, known as the Monroe Doctrine, that "the American continents, by the free and independent condition which they have assumed and maintain, are henceforth not to be considered as subjects for future colonization by any European powers."[144]

Before being elected to the presidency, both Jefferson and Monroe contributed much in public service. Each man had served as governor of Virginia, on diplomatic missions to France, and as secretary of state, and in other ways supported the rising American republic. At the same time, they shared a personal friendship that enriched not only the lives of both men, but also their service to their country. Their names are fittingly linked together in the history of the United States during the critical early years of the young nation.

Notes

1.   Jefferson to Monroe, June 10, 1780, Julian P. Boyd et al., eds. *The Papers of Thomas Jefferson*. 29 vols. to date. (Princeton: Princeton University Press, 1950-), 3:431. Hereafter cited as *Papers*.

2.   Jefferson to Monroe, June 16, 1780, ibid., 3:451-52.

3.   Jefferson to Abner Nash, June 16, 1780, ibid., 3:452.

4.   Monroe to Jefferson, June 26, 1780, ibid., 3:464-66.

5.   Monroe to Jefferson, Sept. 9, 1780, ibid., 3:621-23.

6.   Monroe to Jefferson, Oct. 1, 1781, ibid., 6:124-25.

7.   Jefferson to Monroe, Oct. 5, 1781, ibid., 6:126-28.

8.   Jefferson to Franklin, Adams, and Jay, Oct. 5, 1781, ibid., 6:126.

9.   Monroe to Jefferson, May 11, 1782, ibid., 6:183.

10.   Jefferson to Monroe, May 20, 1782, ibid., 6:186.

11.   James A. Bear, Jr., and Lucia Stanton, eds., *Jefferson's Memorandum Books, 1767-1826* (Princeton: Princeton University Press, 1997), 547; *Papers*, 7:240. Vatell, Emerich de (1714-67), Swiss philosopher and jurist. Chastellux, Francois Jean, marquis de (1734-88) French author and soldier in Seven Years War and American Revolution. Diderot, Denis (1713-84), French encyclopedist, philosopher, and writer. Blackstone, Sir William (1720-80), English jurist. Tissot, Clement Joseph, author of book on military medicine, published in Paris in 1779.

12.   Jefferson to Madison, May 8, 1784, James Morton Smith, ed., *The Republic of Letters: The Correspondence between Thomas Jefferson and James Madison 1776-1826*. 3 vols. (New York: W. W. Norton & Company, 1995), 1:316.

13.   Monroe to Jefferson, May 25, 1784, *Papers*, 7:292.

14.   Monroe to Jefferson, July 20, 1784, ibid., 381.

15.   Ibid.

16.   Jefferson to Monroe, Nov. 11, 1784, ibid., 508.

17.   Jefferson to Monroe, Dec. 11, 1785, ibid., 9:95.

18.   Jefferson to Monroe, Nov. 11, 1784, ibid., 7:512.

19.   Jefferson to Monroe, March 18, 1785, ibid., 8:43.

20.   Jefferson to Monroe, June 17, 1785, ibid., 8:229.

21 Ibid., 8:233.

22 Jefferson to Madison, Dec. 8, 1784, ibid., 7:559.

23 Monroe to Jefferson, May 11, 1786, ibid., 9:511.

24 Jefferson to Monroe, July 9, 1786, ibid., 10:114-15.

25 Jefferson to Monroe, Aug. 11, 1786, ibid., 225.

26 Monroe to Jefferson, Aug. 19, 1786, ibid., 277.

27 Jefferson to Monroe, Dec. 18, 1786, ibid., 612.

28 Monroe to Jefferson, July 27, 1787, ibid., 11:630.

29 Jefferson to Monroe, Aug. 9, 1788, ibid., 13:490.

30 Ibid., 489.

31 Monroe to Jefferson, Feb. 15, 1789, ibid., 14:558.

32 Noble E. Cunningham, Jr., *In Pursuit of Reason: The Life of Thomas Jefferson* (Baton Rouge: Louisiana State University Press, 1987), 123-27.

33 Jefferson's younger daughter, Maria, had joined Jefferson in Paris in July 1787, when she was almost nine years of age.

34 Jefferson to Monroe, June 20, 1790, *Papers*, 16:536-37.

35 Jefferson to Monroe, July 11, 1790, ibid., 17:25.

36 Monroe to Jefferson, Oct. 22, Nov. 26, 1790, ibid., 17:621-22; 18:81; Jefferson to Monroe, Nov. 7. 1790, ibid., 18, 29-30.

37 Monroe to Jefferson, June 17, 1791, ibid., 20:556-57.

38 Monroe to Jefferson, July 17, 1792, ibid., 24:236-37.

39 Jefferson to Monroe, March 11, 1794, ibid., 28:34-35.

40 Monroe to Jefferson, March 3, 1794, ibid., 28:29.

41 Monroe to Jefferson, May 27, 1794, ibid., 28:86-87.

42 Monroe to James Madison, Sept. 2, 1794, Stanislaus Murray Hamilton, ed., *The Writings of James Monroe.* 7 vols. (New York: G. P. Putnam's Sons, 1898-1903; reprint, New York: AMS Press, 1969), 2:37. Hereafter cited as *Monroe Writings*.

43 Monroe to Jefferson, Sept. 7, 1794, *Papers*, 28:145.

44 Jefferson to Monroe, May 26, 1795, ibid., 359-60.

45 Ibid.

46 Monroe to Jefferson, June 27, 1795, ibid., 391.

47 Ibid., 28:392-98.

48 Monroe to Jefferson, Nov. 18, 1795, ibid., 28:527-29.

49 Monroe to Jefferson, July 30, 1796, ibid., 29:161.

50 Monroe to Madison, Jan. 8, 1797, *Monroe Writings*, 3:63-65.

51 Gallatin to his wife, June 28, 30, 1797, Henry Adams, *The Life of Albert Gallatin* (Philadelphia: J. B. Lippincott & Co., 1879; reprint, New York: Peter Smith, 1943), 186-87.

52 Jefferson to Philip Mazzei, April 24, 1796, *Papers*, 29:82.

53 Monroe to Jefferson, July 12, 1797, ibid., 29: 478; Cunningham, *In Pursuit of Reason*, 208-209.

54 James Monroe, *A View of the Conduct of the Executive in the Foreign Affairs of the United States Connected with the Mission to the French Republic During the Years 1794, 5, & 6* (Philadelphia: Benjamin Franklin Bache, 1797).

55 Jefferson to Monroe, Dec. 27, 1797, *Papers*, 29:593-94.

56 Monroe to Jefferson, Feb. 19, 25, April 8, 1798, *Monroe Writings*, 3:104-5, 118.

57 Monroe to Jefferson, June 1, 1798, ibid., 3:125.

58 Jefferson to Monroe, Jan. 23, 1799, Paul L. Ford, ed., *The Works of Thomas Jefferson*, Federal Edition. 12 vols. (New York: G. P. Putnam's Sons, 1904), 9:12. Hereafter cited as Ford.

59 Jefferson to Monroe, Feb. 11, 1799, ibid., 9:36.

60 Monroe to Jefferson, April 23, 1800, *Monroe Writings*, 3:173.

61 Harry Ammon, *James Monroe: The Quest for National Identity* (New York: McGraw-Hill, Inc., 1971), 185-89; Monroe to Jefferson, Sept. 9, 1800, *Monroe Writings*, 3:205.

62 Monroe to Jefferson, Sept. 15, 1800, ibid., 3:208.

63 Jefferson to Monroe, Sept. 20, 1800, Ford, 9:145-46.

64 Jefferson to Monroe, Nov. 24, 1801, Andrew A. Lipscomb and Albert Ellery Bergh, eds., *The Writings of Thomas Jefferson*, Memorial Edition. 20 vols. (Washington, D.C.: Thomas Jefferson Memorial Association, 1904), 10:294-98. Hereafter cited as L&B.

65 Jefferson to Monroe, Feb. 15, 1801, ibid., 10:202.

66 Monroe to Jefferson, Jan. 27, 1801, Jefferson Papers, Library of Congress.

67 Noble E. Cunningham, Jr., "Election of 1800," in Arthur M. Schlesinger, Jr. and Fred Israel, eds., *History of American Presidential Elections*. 4 vols. (New York: Chelsea

House Publishers, McGraw-Hill Book Co., 1971), 1:132-33, 237.

68 Monroe to Jefferson, March 18, 1801, *Monroe Writings*, 3:269.

69 Monroe to Madison, March 11, 1801, Robert J. Brugger, et al., eds., *The Papers of James Madison: Secretary of State Series*. 5 vols. to date. (Charlottesville: University Press of Virginia, 1986-), 1:11.

70 Monroe to Jefferson, May 4, 1801, *Monroe Writings*, 3:282-83.

71 Jefferson to Monroe, May 29, 1801, Ford, 9:261-62.

72 Jefferson to Thomas Mann Randolph, Jr., June 18, 1801, Jefferson Papers, Library of Congress.

73 Jefferson to Monroe, June 20, 1801, James Monroe Papers, Library of Congress, microfilm edition. See also Noble E. Cunningham, Jr., *The Process of Government under Jefferson* (Princeton: Princeton University Press, 1978), 22.

74 Monroe to Jefferson, June 20, 1801, *Monroe Writings*, 3:298-99.

75 Madison to Monroe, July 25, 1801, Brugger, et al., *The Papers of James Madison*, 1:477.

76 Monroe to Jefferson, Dec. 21, 1801, *Monroe Writings*, 3:323.

77 Monroe to Jefferson, April 25, 1802, ibid, 3:343.

78 Jefferson to Monroe, Jan. 10, 1803, Ford, 9:416-17.

79 Jefferson to Robert R. Livingston, April 18, 1802, ibid., 9:364-65.

80 Jefferson to Monroe, Jan. 13. 1803, L&B, 10:344.

81 Cunningham, *In Pursuit of Reason*, 264.

82 Jefferson to Monroe, March 21, 1807, L&B, 11:170.

83 Jefferson to Monroe, May 29, 1807, ibid., 11:211-12.

84 Jefferson to Monroe, Feb. 18, 1808, Ford, 11:10-11.

85 Monroe to Jefferson, Feb. 27, 1808, *Monroe Writings*, 5:24-25.

86 Ibid., 5:26.

87 Jefferson to Monroe, March 10, 1808, L&B, 12:8.

88 Monroe to Jefferson, Jan. 18, 1809, *Monroe Writings*, 5:90-91.

89 Jefferson to Monroe, Jan. 28, 1809, Ford, 11:96.

90 Jefferson to Madison, March 30, 1809, Robert A. Rutland, et al., eds., *The Papers of James Madison: Presidential Series*. 4 vols. (Charlottesville: University Press of Virginia, 1984), 1:91.

[91] Jefferson to Madison, Nov. 30, 1809, Ford, 11:127.

[92] Ammon, *Monroe: Quest for National Identity*, 281; Monroe to Jefferson, April 3, 1811, *Monroe Writings*, 5:184-85.

[93] Ammon, *Monroe: Quest for National Identity*, 286-87.

[94] Jefferson to Monroe, May 5, 1811, Ford, 11:206.

[95] See J.C.A. Stagg, *Mr. Madison's War: Politics, Diplomacy, and Warfare in the Early American Republic, 1783-1830* (Princeton: Princeton University Press, 1983).

[96] Monroe to Jefferson, June 7, 1813, *Monroe Writings*, 5:259-60.

[97] Monroe to Jefferson, June 7, 1813, Jefferson Papers, Library of Congress.

[98] Ibid.

[99] Jefferson to Monroe, May 30, 1813, L&B, 13:251.

[100] Monroe to Jefferson, June 16, 1813, *Monroe's Writings*, 5:269.

[101] Jefferson to Monroe, June 18, 1813, L&B, 13:262.

[102] Jefferson to Monroe, Sept. 24, 1814, Ford, 11:430-31.

[103] Monroe to Jefferson, Oct. 4, 1814, *Monroe Writings*, 5:298-99.

[104] Monroe to Jefferson, Oct. 10, 1814, ibid., 5:299.

[105] Monroe to Jefferson, Dec. 21, 1814, ibid., 5:303-306.

[106] Jefferson to Monroe, Jan. 1, 1815, Ford, 11:442-46.

[107] Monroe to Jefferson, Feb. 15, 1815, Jefferson Papers, Library of Congress. Henry Carroll was Henry Clay's personal secretary. See also Donald R. Hickey, *The War of 1812* (Urbana: University of Illinois Press, 1989), 297.

[108] Jefferson to Monroe, Feb. 17, 1816, Jefferson Papers, Library of Congress.

[109] Jefferson to Monroe, Oct. 16, 1816, ibid.

[110] Jefferson to Monroe, Jan. 10, 1817, ibid.

[111] Monroe to Jefferson, Feb. 23, 1817, *Monroe Writings*, 6:2-4.

[112] Jefferson to Monroe, April 8, 1817, Jefferson Papers, Library of Congress.

[113] Jefferson to Monroe, April 13, 1817, ibid.

[114] Monroe to Jefferson, April 23, 1817, *Monroe Writings*, 6:21-22.

[115] John Adams to Jefferson, May 26, 1817, Lester J. Capon, ed., *The Adams-Jefferson Letters: The Complete Correspondence Between Thomas Jefferson and Abigail and John Adams* (Chapel Hill: University of North Carolina Press, 1959), 517.

[116] Monroe to Jefferson, July 27, 1817, ibid., 6:26-29.

[117] Monroe to Jefferson, Dec. 23, 1817, ibid., 6:47.

[118] Monroe to Jefferson, Oct. 3, 1818, Jefferson Papers, Library of Congress.

[119] Jefferson to Monroe, Jan. 18, 1819, Ford, 12:113.

[120] Noble E. Cunningham, Jr., *The Presidency of James Monroe* (Lawrence: University Press of Kansas, 1996), 68-69.

[121] Monroe to Jefferson, Feb. 7, 1820, *Monroe Writings*, 6:113-14.

[122] Monroe to Jefferson, Feb. 19, 1820, ibid., 6:116.

[123] Jefferson to Monroe, March 3, 1820, Jefferson Papers, Library of Congress.

[124] Cunningham, *Presidency of James Monroe*, 102-3.

[125] Jefferson to John Holmes, April 22, 1820, Ford, 12:158.

[126] Jefferson to Monroe, May 14, 1820, ibid., 12:160.

[127] Monroe to Jefferson, Aug. 2, 1820, *Monroe Writings*, 6:144-45. John W. Forbes was appointed minister to Buenos Aires.

[128] Jefferson to Monroe, Aug. 13, 1821, Jefferson Papers, Library of Congress.

[129] Monroe to Jefferson, Sept. 6, 1821, *Monroe Writings*, 6:192.

[130] Monroe to Jefferson, Nov. 25, 1822, ibid., 6:298.

[131] Jefferson to William Short, March 28, 1823, Ford, 12:283.

[132] Monroe to Jefferson, June 2, 1823, *Monroe Writings*, 6:308-11.

[133] Jefferson to Monroe, June 11, 1823, Ford, 12:291-93.

[134] Monroe to Jefferson, Oct. 17, 1823, *Monroe Writings*, 6:323-25.

[135] Jefferson to Monroe, Oct. 24, 1823, Ford, 12:318-21.

[136] Fred Israel, ed., *The State of the Union Messages of the Presidents, 1790-1966*. 3 vols. (New York: Chelsea House Publishers, R. R. Bowker Company, 1967), 1:204.

[137] Ibid., 212-13. On the Monroe Doctrine see Ernest R. May, *The Making of the Monroe Doctrine* (Cambridge: Harvard University Press, 1975).

[138] Monroe to Madison, March 27, 1824, *Monroe Writings*, 7:18.

[139] Monroe to Jefferson, Aug. 26, 1824, ibid., 7:34-35; Dumas Malone, *Jefferson and His Time*. 6 vols. (Boston: Little, Brown, & Company, 1948-81), 6:450-51.

[140] Cunningham, *In Pursuit of Reason*, 344.

141 W. P. Cresson, *James Monroe* (Chapel Hill: University of North Carolina Press, 1946), 473-74.

142 Monroe to Jefferson, Feb. 23, 1826, *Monroe Writings*, 7:69-70.

143 Jefferson to Monroe, March 8, 1826, Jefferson Papers, Library of Congress.

144 Monroe's seventh annual message to Congress, Dec. 2, 1823, Israel, ed., *The State of the Union Messages of the Presidents*, 1:204.

Bibliographical Note

Sources for the study of Thomas Jefferson and of James Monroe are extensive and include the following:

Bear, James A., Jr., and Lucia C. Stanton, eds., *Jefferson's Memorandum Books, 1767-1826*. Princeton: Princeton University Press, 1987.

Boyd, Julian P., et al., eds., *The Papers of Thomas Jefferson*. 29 vols. to date, covering through 1797. Princeton: Princeton University Press, 1950- .

Ford, Paul L., ed., *The Works of Thomas Jefferson*. 12 vols. Federal Edition. New York, 1904.

Hamilton, Stanislaus M., *The Writings of James Monroe*. 7 vols. New York, 1898-1902; reprint edition, New York, AMS Press, 1969.

Lipscomb, Andrew A., and Albert E. Bergh, eds., *The Writings of Thomas Jefferson*. 20 vols. Washington, D.C., 1903-1904.

Rutland, Robert A., et al., eds., *The Papers of James Madison: Secretary of State Series*. Charlottesville, University Press of Virginia, 1986- .

Smith, James Morton, ed., *The Republic of Letters: The Correspondence of Thomas Jefferson and James Madison, 1776-1826*. 3 vols. New York: W. W. Norton, 1995.

Major collections of the manuscript letters and other papers of both Jefferson and Monroe are in the Manuscripts Division of the Library of Congress and are available on microfilm.

The most detailed biography of Thomas Jefferson is Dumas Malone, *Jefferson and His Time*, 6 vols. (Boston: Little, Brown & Company, 1948-81). Other scholarly biographies include Merrill D. Peterson, *Thomas Jefferson and the New Nation* (New York: Oxford University Press, 1970), and Noble E. Cunningham, Jr., *In Pursuit of Reason: The Life of Thomas Jefferson* (Baton Rouge: Louisiana State University Press, 1987).

The major biography of James Monroe is Harry Ammon, *James Monroe: The Quest for National Identity* (New York: McGraw-Hill, Inc., 1971). An earlier biography is W. P. Cresson, *James Monroe* (Chapel Hill: University of North Carolina Press, 1946. Monroe's presidential years are treated in Noble E. Cunningham, Jr., *The Presidency of James Monroe* (Lawrence: University Press of Kansas, 1996).

Other related works include: Ernest R. May, *The Making of the Monroe Doctrine* (Cambridge: Harvard University Press, 1975); Alexander DeConde, *This Affair of Louisiana* (New York: Charles Scribner's Sons, 1976); Burton Spivak, *Jefferson's English Crisis: Commerce, Embargo, and the Republican Revolution* (Charlottesville: University Press of

Virginia, 1979); Robert A. Rutland, *The Presidency of James Madison* (Lawrence: University Press of Kansas, 1990); J.C.A. Stagg, *Mr. Madison's War: Politics, Diplomacy, and Warfare in the Early Republic, 1783-1830* (Princeton: Princeton University Press, 1983); Daniel P. Jordan, *Political Leadership in Jefferson's Virginia* (Charlottesville: University Press of Virginia, 1983); William Earl Weeks, *John Quincy Adams and American Global Empire* (Lexington: University Press of Kentucky, 1992); Noble E. Cunningham, Jr., *The Process of Government under Jefferson* (Princeton: Princeton University Press, 1978); Ralph Louis Ketcham, *Presidents Above Parties: The First American Presidency, 1789-1829* (Chapel Hill: University of North Carolina Press, for the Institute of Early American History and Culture, Williamsburg, Va., 1984); James Roger Sharp, *American Politics in the Early Republic: The New Nation in Crisis* (New Haven: Yale University Press, 1993); Noble E. Cunningham, Jr., *The Inaugural Addresses of President Thomas Jefferson, 1801 and 1805* (Columbia: University of Missouri Press, 2001).

INDEX